IBM SPSS

Comprehensive Beginners Guide to Learn Statistics using IBM SPSS from A-Z

© Copyright 2019 - All rights reserved.

The content contained within this book may not be reproduced, duplicated or transmitted without direct written permission from the author or the publisher.

Under no circumstances will any blame or legal responsibility be held against the publisher, or author, for any damages, reparation, or monetary loss due to the information contained within this book. Either directly or indirectly.

Legal Notice:

This book is copyright protected. This book is only for personal use. You cannot amend, distribute, sell, use, quote or paraphrase any part, or the content within this book, without the consent of the author or publisher.

Disclaimer Notice:

Please note the information contained within this document is for educational and entertainment purposes only. All effort has been executed to present accurate, up to date, and reliable, complete information. No warranties of any kind are declared or implied. Readers acknowledge that the author is not engaging in the rendering of legal, financial, medical or professional advice. The content within this book has been derived from various sources. Please consult a licensed professional before attempting any techniques outlined in this book.

By reading this document, the reader agrees that under no circumstances is the author responsible for any losses, direct or indirect, which are incurred as a result of the use of information contained within this document, including, but not limited to, — errors, omissions, or inaccuracies.

Table of Contents

Introduction 1

Chapter One: Why Use IBM SPSS? 9
    History 11
    Making the Case for IBM SPSS 14
    In the next chapter... 19

Chapter Two: Installing IBM SPSS v.25 20
    IBM SPSS Installation Walkthrough 21
    Our First Look at IBM SPSS 32
    In the next chapter... 33

Chapter Three: About Data 34
    Why Conduct Data Analysis? 38
    Defining Data 44
    Machine-Readable Data Types 45
    Ordered & Unordered Data 49
    Is there a process for Data Analysis? 51
    A Note on Research Methods 52
    The Importance of Cleaning Data for Analysis 55
    In the next chapter... 57

Chapter Four: The SPSS Data Editor 58
    The Variable List in SPSS 61

The Data Overview Pane.. 67
  Open Multiple Tabs in SPSS 68
  Search for Items.. 69
  Settings & Notifications 70
  New Analysis 71
  Other Useful Tab Functions 72
  In the next chapter... 73

Chapter Five: Introduction to Statistics 74
  A Definition of Statistics.. 77
  Going Late to Work - A Short, Statistical Study 80
  Descriptive Statistics 83
  Inferential Statistics 86
  In the next chapter... 87

Chapter Six: The SPSS Data Editor Menus....................................... 88
  The File Menu 88
  The Data Menu 90
  The Transform Menu 92
  The Analyze Menu 93
  The Visualize Menu 94
  The Utilities Menu... 95
  The Help Menu... 96
  Quick Access to Important Functions 98
  Other Case and Variable Menu Functionality....................... 100
  In the next chapter... 105

Chapter Seven: Descriptive Statistics 106
  Common Applications of Descriptive Statistics 107
  Examining Datasets and their Distribution 109

What Do Descriptive Statistics Measure? 110
Measures of Central Tendency 110
Measures of Spread 114
Measures of Shape 118
The Importance of Using Charts 121
Presenting Descriptive Statistics Using Charts & Graphs 123
In the next chapter… 130

Chapter Eight: Computing Descriptive Statistics using SPSS 131
Frequency 132
Measures of Central Tendency 136
Measures of Spread 149
Measures of Shape or Distribution 157
Using the Case Summaries Section under Reports 164
In the next chapter… 167

Chapter Nine: Creating Charts in SPSS 168
Common Graphs Available in SPSS 169
Other Charts Available in SPSS 197
In the next chapter… 207

Chapter Ten: Introduction to Inferential Statistics 208
Sample, Population, & Random Sampling 210
The Central Limit Theorem 211
Probability Distributions 213
Approaches Used in Inferential Statistics 214
In the next chapter… 216

Chapter Eleven: Using SPSS for Inferential Statistics 217
Estimation 218

    Hypothesis Testing 223

    Other SPSS Features Available in Inferential Statistics 227

    In the next chapter 229

Chapter Twelve: Using SPSS Syntax Commands 230

    Creating and Using Syntax Command Files 232

    In Closing 240

Final Thoughts 241

Bibliography 246

    Academic Texts 246

    Online Sources 246

    Images 256

Introduction

We live in a world where information takes on a life of its own and spreads rapidly. Faster than ever before. For some people, their lives depend on obtaining a steady stream of information as it affects their lives in the most telling ways. The daily news is the simplest example of this phenomenon. It is truly the lifeblood of society and helps us evolve into better informed individuals with every passing day.

As one can tell, information on the whole comes at us from every direction. Its influence on business, politics, and government, banking, the STEM fields, and even the social sciences cannot be understated. But its journey begins with raw data being compiled by means of an experiment or study.

From raw data to processed information

Whether it is the crime rate of certain neighbourhoods, the number of accidents each month in a district, the profit and loss of said company each quarter, the English Premier League table standings, or even the chances of a politician winning the election, all of these data points lead us to drawing broader conclusions that affect our lives in the here and now. That said, data is just as useful in academic research too and impacts the kind of medicines we use, the food we eat, the clothes we wear, and the cars we drive. It's literally everywhere.

Data helped us understand why the 2008 financial recession occurred

In fact, it has become so essential to our lives that data analysis and science is now an important field of study that has evolved on its own merit. Now, as most scientists would admit, the information that we receive on a daily basis hinges on obtaining authentic data. In other words, data that is collected, 'cleaned', analysed, and interpreted accurately. It goes without saying that without a sound framework in place to process data into information, we stand the risk of not being able to make beneficial decisions in every sphere of our lives.

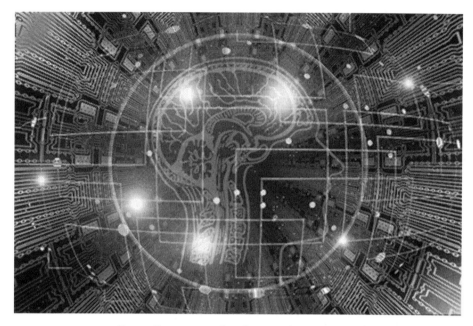

Data Science - the dawn of a new age

This is because data, on its own, does not serve any useful purpose. We, as the researcher, analyst, or scientist, must endeavour to bring it to life.

This begins with using reliable tools and longstanding statistical methods that can help us perform data analysis and interpretation as quickly and accurately as possible. Once we are able to achieve this ideal state of being able to apply the right statistical method to said problem, and are able to obtain results with a powerful tool, we are well on our way to transforming obtained data into trustworthy information.

Data analysis tools aren't everything; statistical methods matter too

So, where do we begin?

I think the first step is to immerse ourselves in a world of numbers and methods to process these numbers. Develop a statistical bent-of-mind, as they call it. Of course, this includes collecting both quantitative and qualitative data through the creation of well-designed experiments.

The second step is to learn the use of certain tools that helps us transform data obtained into crucial findings. This is why we will also look at SPSS.

The third is being able to articulate and present our findings and disseminate them to the right audience, which SPSS makes almost effortless.

Much like SPSS, "Big Blue" has been around for a while

That said, in reading the title of this book, you'd know that this is exactly what we intend to cover as we look at both the study of statistics and the IBM SPSS tool. Of course, we intend to use a variety of simple datasets that can help us understand how to apply statistical concepts, but we will also get some practice in with the SPSS tool.

But that's not all: not only will you know how to use IBM's SPSS, but you will also understand the reason and the context in which these features are applied to any dataset. In doing so, you should be able to use these features in any situation, provided you are able to determine which statistical method is most conducive to solving a certain problem.

The SPSS Logo, prior to being acquired by IBM in 2010

Given the number of features that this tool has at its disposal, it's wise to begin with the absolute basics and gradually build on this foundation as we move from descriptive to inferential statistics. If anything, IBM SPSS has features that go well beyond the topic of descriptive statistics that almost every adult has learned in high school. So, you can imagine the capability that you will possess at your disposal once you have understood how to use this tool's features and why. The creators of this package developed this tool for that very purpose.

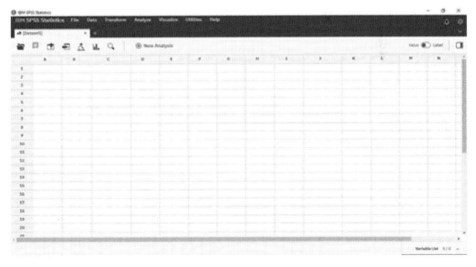

An Empty Data file in SPSS v. 25

In saying that, this book should serve as a reference guide for those who wish to go beyond the basics into territory that requires a solid understanding of advanced statistical concepts. Still, as a beginner, it will be wise to move forward with care so that you solidify your understanding before you begin to use these advanced methods.

Finally, even if the subject matter is a bit deep, don't be so serious that you forget to have fun with both the SPSS tool and the study of statistics on the whole.

Having said that, let's get to crunching numbers without any further delay!

Chapter One

Why Use IBM SPSS?

Ever since mathematical statistics became a field of study, statisticians had to gather, compute, and present their research findings manually. Statistics have been around for centuries, but what was yet to be invented was a method by which all the tasks, right from data gathering to presentation, were executed quickly.

Karl Pearson - The Father of Statistics

Can you imagine how long it would have taken? To not only collect data, select a sample, and analyse it, but also compute the results for presentation too?

Quite clearly, statisticians were very aware of the far-reaching impacts that their experiments could have in the development of society as a whole. What would be the point of conducting extensive research if they didn't have a tool that could help them manage large amounts of data? Or even help them compute the results quickly?

Imagine using "card punchers" in the New Millennium! Whew, no thanks!

For example, it's hard to imagine how researchers collected and stored information when it was time for the decennial Census in the United States. Even if it was just to compute the current population across the country.

History

It wouldn't be long before all this would change. 1968 was that year. Three Stanford University students from very different professional backgrounds put their talents together to come up with the Statistical Package for the Social Sciences. Now remembered as Norman H. Nie, C. Hadlai Hull, and Dale H. Bent who developed SPSS, they are widely recognized as pioneers of the idea that being able to process raw data into information could drive decision-making so as to benefit us as a whole.

The genesis of SPSS begins with these three individuals who wanted to process large amounts of social science data that was collected using different methods of research. While Nie offered his expertise as a social scientist, Bent developed the SPSS file system structure. Hull put it all together by developing the package itself using his programming skills.

Hull used the FORTRAN programming language to create SPSS

It wouldn't be long before SPSS would become a corporation in 1975 while continuing to cater to clientele who found it easy to port the code to their mainframe computers. With the dawn of the age of the PC, SPSS would be the first corporation to market a statistical software package for MS-DOS and Windows. Last but not least, SPSS would move into the predictive analytics market segment.

As most people know, predictive analytics help you obtain knowledge from the past by data analysis which is used to predict the future and thus improve outcomes in a number of ways. As mentioned earlier, this segment goes back to the initial goal of improving decision-making by the intelligent analysis of data.

Four Types of Business Analytics

Seeing the potential, IBM then decided to acquire SPSS for the value of $1.2 billion in 2009 and by October 2010 the software package commonly known as SPSS was now called IBM SPSS. It is now one of the key brands in IBM's Business Analytics Portfolio.

IBM acquired SPSS in 2009

Making the Case for IBM SPSS

Given a plethora of software packages that are available, one might wonder why they should pick SPSS amongst the lot. Why not use the R programming language that has been designed precisely for statistical analysis by two New Zealand professors?

Python and R are popular languages for Data Science

Or even MATLAB? Or even the popular Python libraries such NumPy, SciPy, PANDAS, and Matplotlib? There's even an open source version of SPSS called PSPP that works as a free alternative.

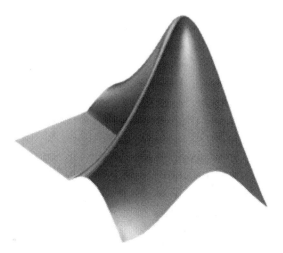

Why not MATLAB?

While each of these offerings are worthy competitors, one must add that SPSS is just simple to use. It has features for both beginners and very experienced users that you will not find elsewhere. In other words, key in and save your data, process it, and generate the results. Better still, you can export data into SPSS from a variety of formats. It's as simple as that.

A CSV file opened in Notepad (CSV stands for comma separated values)

Better still, you don't need any programming knowledge apart from being able to point-and-click with your mouse. If you understand how to use the command line or Terminal in Windows or Linux, that should be enough to work with SPSS Syntax.

So, while it is vital to learn Python and R in order to pursue a career in Data Science, SPSS serves as an excellent starting point for beginners. With a graphical user interface and a variety of powerful features, this is the perfect statistics package for researchers with or without programming knowledge.

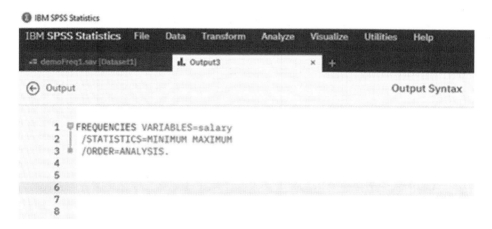

IBM SPSS Syntax - Example

If that's the case, then why not just use Microsoft Excel instead of SPSS? At first glance, the SPSS default screen looks like a spreadsheet, doesn't it? What's the difference anyway?

All fair questions to ask, quite honestly. While Excel allows for the user to key in, store, and manipulate data, these features exist in SPSS but there's so much more. Given how SPSS was developed particularly for the statistical analysis of data, you can perform complex statistical calculations. In stark contrast, Excel is yet to include these functions.

Student ID	Student Name	English	Maths	Science	Subject Average
0001	Willie Osbourne	79	88	59	75.33
0002	Silvia Short	65	92	55	70.67
0003	Larry Crivello	86	95	82	87.67
0004	Trinity Schuller	71	97	79	82.33
0005	Troy Hayworth	77	83	81	80.33
0006	Felton Musso	90	96	83	89.67
0007	Brock Shanley	72	75	79	75.33
0008	Beulah Jaynes	83	85	80	82.67
0009	Alison Singer	62	74	67	67.67
0010	Melissa Doonan	70	79	79	76.00
0011	Marco Reus	99	85	90	91.33
0012	Kevin de Bruyne	86	72	92	83.33
0013	Emiliano Sala	71	83	89	81.00
0014	Lionel Messi	82	99	88	89.67
0015	Diego Costa	79	88	84	83.67
0016	Cristiano Ronaldo	85	85	79	83.00
0017	Fernando Torres	90	81	88	86.33
0018	Kylian Mbappe	88	79	90	85.67
0019	Neymar	78	91	83	84.00
0020	Luis Suarez	99	99	86	94.67
	Class Averages	80.6	86.3	80.65	

Excel works for simple data analysis but SPSS can do much more

For example, while performing a cluster analysis in SPSS might be effortless, you'll need add-ons if you want to perform this calculation in Excel. In other words, the more complex the statistical calculation, you're just better off using SPSS. That's exactly what it was designed for.

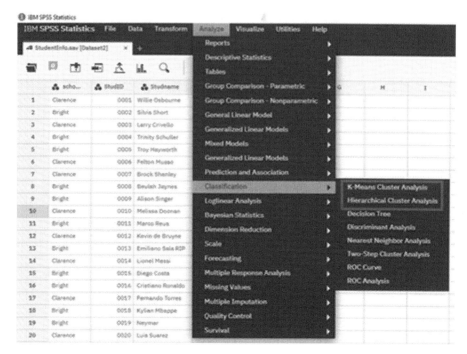

Performing a cluster analysis using SPSS

But that's not all: speaking of add-ons, one can even extend the functionality of SPSS to include Python macros that helps you automate all your data processing tasks. How cool? Finally, there's an Extension Hub with an ever-increasing number of extensions that help you build the SPSS syntax too.

```
1   get file 'histobar.sav'
2
3   BEGIN PROGRAM
4   import spss
5   for i in range(286,301):
6       spss.Submit("'XGRAPH CHART = [HISTOBAR] BY v%d[s] /COORDINATE SPLIT = YES'"%i)
7   END PROGRAM
8
9   frequencies all
```

A Python macro in SPSS - Example

So, to sum things up, SPSS is just right for the normal user who might not have much programming knowledge but has a solid understanding of statistical theory and needs to have capability to run a wide variety of statistical calculations at his disposal.

Of course, with IBM now owning this product, you can expect excellent support for a stable product that has stood the test of time. That said, it should come as no surprise that SPSS is considered to be the leading software package used for statistical analysis by several other businesses for over half a century now.

In the next chapter...

Now that we've been introduced to the history, purpose, and the use of SPSS, it's time to get some hands-on experience with SPSS itself. That begins with installing the SPSS package from the IBM website, which is what we will look at in the next chapter.

Chapter Two

Installing IBM SPSS v.25

Software doesn't ever stay the same. There's always the need to fix bugs or add new features based on customer requests. Even if SPSS offers a comprehensive set of features for the statistician, there are still improvements that need to take place. Currently, the latest version of SPSS that you can obtain is version 25 that was released in August 2017. This is what we will use as we advance through this course on statistics for beginners.

The SPSS Welcome Page

So, where do we begin? As someone who knows nothing about SPSS? You'll find several sites over the internet that allow you to download this software. Either you can purchase the software immediately or you can try it for a period of 14 days.

IBM SPSS Installation Walkthrough

Now, no matter which site you wish to begin your SPSS download from, it'll direct you to the IBM page immediately. This is because you will have to open an IBM account first. Whether you download either the trial version or decide to purchase the software immediately, this step is mandatory.

Step 1: Enter Correct Information in the Fields Below

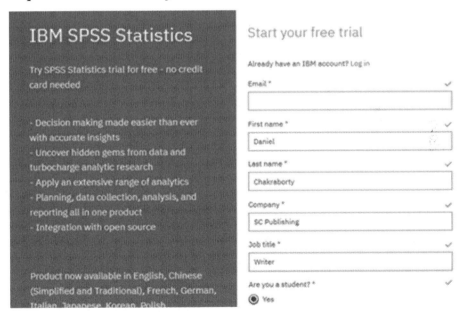

Create your IBM account

Upon completion of this step, you will have to wait for a seven-digit code that will be sent to the email that you use in the registration process.

Step 2: Key in the seven-digit code received at the registered email

Check your email

For your security, we need to verify your identity. We sent a 7-digit code to
Please enter it below.

Enter 7 digit code

Verify

Enter the seven-digit code that you received in your email

Once you do, an IBM account will be created for you, for which you will receive a notification at the registered email. This is the IBM id that you will have to use from now on. Your IBM SPSS trial begins from that very moment and lasts for about 14 days in all. Unless you intend to purchase a copy of SPSS right away.

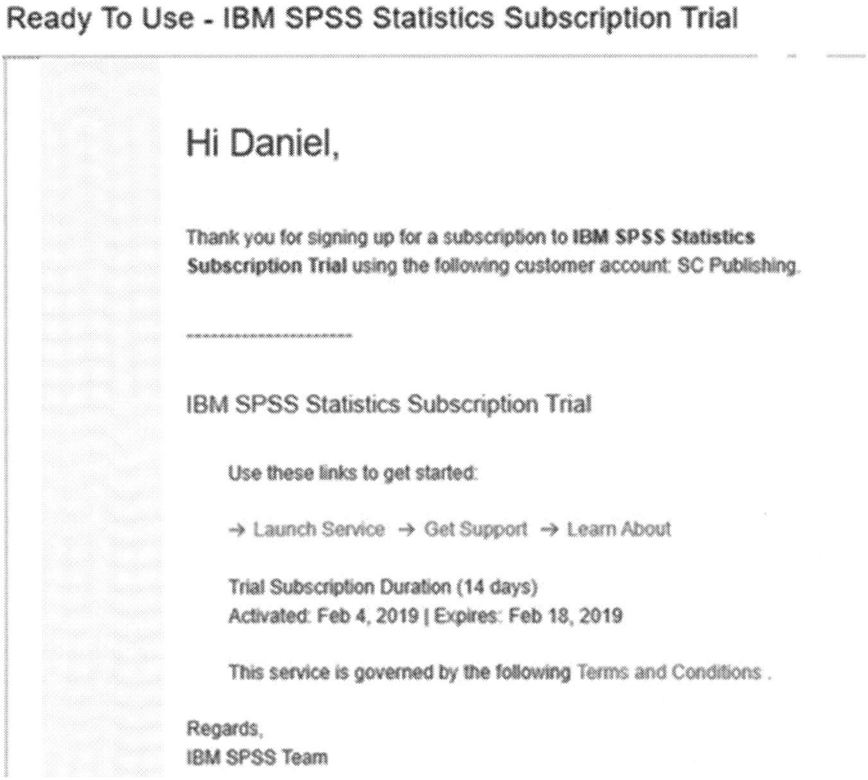

Ready To Use - IBM SPSS Statistics Subscription Trial

Hi Daniel,

Thank you for signing up for a subscription to **IBM SPSS Statistics Subscription Trial** using the following customer account: SC Publishing.

IBM SPSS Statistics Subscription Trial

Use these links to get started:

→ Launch Service → Get Support → Learn About

Trial Subscription Duration (14 days)
Activated: Feb 4, 2019 | Expires: Feb 18, 2019

This service is governed by the following Terms and Conditions.

Regards,
IBM SPSS Team

On receiving this email, your SPSS 14-day trial begins

Step 3: Log into your IBM account using the email and password entered during registration.

After logging into your IBM account, select "Download"

You'll find yourself on a page located within your IBM account that invites you to download SPSS. As you can see, your trial period is statused "Active".

Finally, select the "Download" option in order to move to the next page where you can obtain an .exe file for installation.

Step 4: Select 'Download' to use either the Classic or the latest version of IBM SPSS.

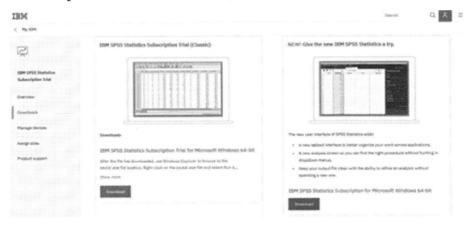

Select either Classic or the latest SPSS version, and hit "Download"

Once you've reached the next page, you can either download the Classic or the trial version of IBM SPSS. IBM determines your system specifications and provides you with a download file that would run best on your system

Still, before you do anything else, take a look at the table below in order to understand the minimum system requirements in order to install and run SPSS without issues.

Operating System	Windows: Version 8, 8.1 & 10 Apple: OS X Yosemite Linux: Red Hat Enterprise 6 & 7, Ubuntu 14.04 and 16.04.
Hardware	2 GHz or higher
Memory	4 GB RAM (4 GB+ for better results)
Disk Space	2 GB or more

Now, once you're certain that you can run SPSS without a problem on your system, select "Download". Depending on your internet connection, you'll have to wait for some time as the .exe file is almost 1 GB in size.

Step 5: Right-click and run the executable file to commence installation.

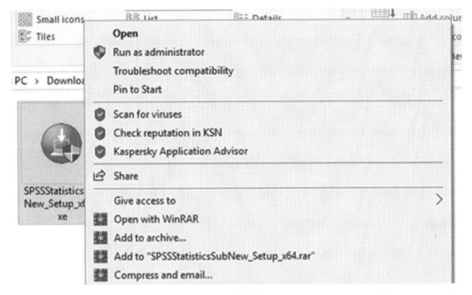

Select either Classic or the latest SPSS version, and hit "Download"

As shown below, this is how the IBM SPSS icon looks, no matter which operating system you use.

The IBM SPSS Icon

Windows users can find the IBM SPSS executable file in the Downloads folder.

Step 6: Select the green checkbox next to "I Agree" and "Continue".

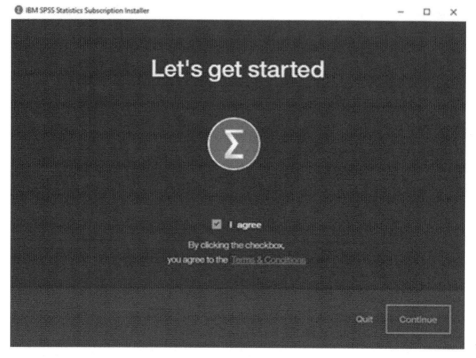

Select the "I Agree" Checkbox and the Continue option.

If you want to read the Terms & Conditions first before completing the installation, feel free to by selecting the green hyperlink below the checkbox.

Step 7: Select a drive and folder to save all your SPSS files.

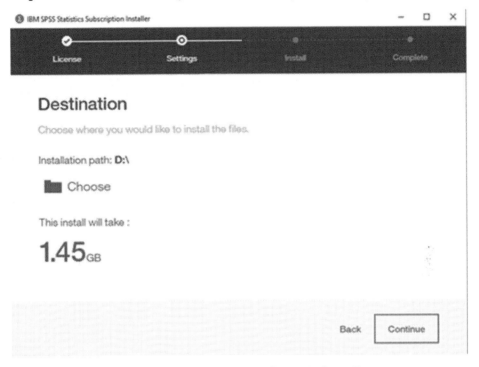

Select the installation path or drive. Select Continue.

As you can see, the SPSS installation will take about 1.45 GB of space. Also, you will find the progress bar towards the completion of installation in the upper portion of your screen.

Select Continue to move to the next step.

Step 8: Wait for the installer to complete the SPSS Installation.

Wait for the "Installation Complete" page, and select Launch

Once the progress bar indicates that the installation is complete, select Launch. We're almost there!

Step 9: Login with your IBM id and password.

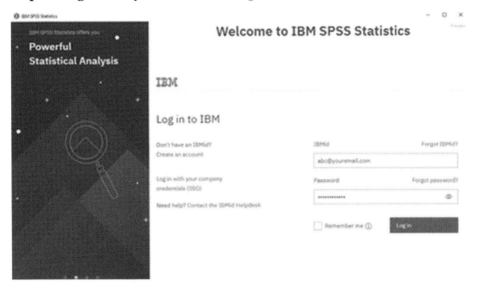

Log in with your IBM id credentials

This step, which involves entering your IBM id details, is mandatory. You will not be able to use SPSS if you skip this step. Since your IBM account has information on whether you are using a trial or paid version, you'll have access to SPSS until your trial period or monthly subscription expires.

Our First Look at IBM SPSS

Welcome to SPSS! The installation is complete and was hopefully simple enough to follow! Be patient and wait for SPSS package to load. It might a little time, depending on your system specifications.

The SPSS Welcome Page

Now, once you get past the splash page that welcomes you to using SPSS in your own language, you'll get to a page that asks you select a dataset, pick a sample, or create a new Syntax file.

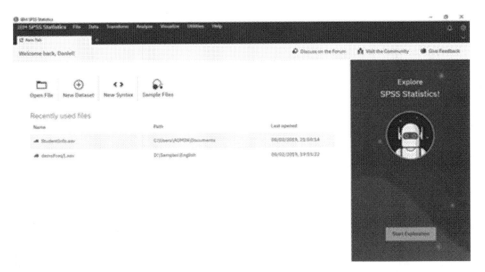

Your First Look at SPSS

If you select New Dataset, we'll be on our way to creating our very first. Of course, you can always look at a number of samples that SPSS has prepared and which would be useful since you'll get to see how the variables and cases are laid out for analysis.

In the next chapter...

Now that we've completed the IBM SPSS installation and have had our first look at the layout of the statistics package, let's move on to the next chapter where we examine key concepts and standards related to the nature of data itself.

Chapter Three

About Data

Whether we realise this or not, data is everywhere. Our five senses take in data every day while our mind processes this data into patterns from which we can draw conclusions.

For example, if we come into contact with something sharp or hot, would we knowingly perform the same action again? Of course not. This is because our mind has recorded the burning or painful sensation. It's sensory data. Going forward, we remember that experience and do everything we can to never repeat it. Not unless we care about our physical health.

Don't touch the stove!

In stark contrast, when we eat chocolate or exercise, we get that gentle high. This is also sensory data. We enjoy these activities because we're reminded of that sense of pleasure and we interpret this as good.

But what does this have to do with the study of data analytics? A lot, actually.

Computers also accept data and are 'conditioned' by code to carry out certain actions. For example, we might want to find the average of a set of numbers, as shown in the Python code below:

```python
#Calculate the average of all numbers in a given list
myList = [234, 755, 112, 89, 65, 678, 351, 492, 585, 825, 963, 1063]
total = 0
for i in range(0,len(myList)):
    total = total + myList[i]

avList = total/len(myList)
print("The list to be processed is", myList)
print("The average of the list is: ", avList)
```

Calculating the average of numbers on a list

When you run this simple snippet of Python code, you get desirable output as shown below:

```
Python 3.6.1 (default, Dec 2015, 13:05:11)
[GCC 4.8.2] on linux
The list to be processed is [234, 755, 112, 89, 65, 678, 351, 4
92, 585, 825, 963, 1063]
The average of the list is:  517.6666666666666
```

Output - Calculated Average of Python List

In the example above, the numbers enclosed within the square brackets can be likened to a single variable of data. As simple as this example is, one can enter several variables of data into a statistical package like SPSS. You really don't have to write code or do anything apart from processing the data with the features available.

Now, very differently from humans, computers take in this data in a structured, machine-readable format and execute the code as instructed. One must thank Konrad Zuse for attempting to create the first workable computer using the universal language of 1s and 0s.

Konrad Zuse - Inventor of the Programmable Computer

Using the example above, each of the numbers within the square brackets is converted to its binary equivalent and then processed. This is the only language that machines can comprehend and respond to these days, unlike humans who can easily derive meaning from a block of text, a piece of artwork, or even someone's tone of voice or body language. Of course, this is until artificial intelligence begins to rival that of ours, but that's a discussion for another day.

When will we achieve technological singularity?

What is being pointed out here is the difference between human-readable and machine-readable data. While the former can interpret subjective non-numeric data almost effortlessly, the latter is restricted to processing structured, numeric data (or non-numeric data transformed into its numeric equivalent) so that we can draw accurate conclusions about the problem we wish to solve.

Computers cannot derive meaning from text, pictures, and video as humans do

Considering the aforementioned restrictions, what's the point of conducting data analysis anyway? Luckily, there exists a variety of sources in the real world from which we can capture and quantify this data. Better still, computers can help us process large amounts of data and increase the effectiveness of our analysis.

That said, in being able to understand the difference between these forms of data captured, one should understand that the form in which we collect data should be conducive to the tools we use to process it.

Why Conduct Data Analysis?

Given that there's a lot of hype about Data Science and the art of carrying out data analysis, one might wonder if this actually happens. Are there specific instances where gleaning insights from data analysis has impacted our lives positively? Or is data analysis just a whole bunch of nerd-speak reserved for a certain group of people with high IQs? To dumbfound and obfuscate the rest of the population with pretentious jargon.

Data analysis has nothing to do with being nerdy

Hardly.

Don't take my word for it. To answer that question fully, let's look at a few real world problems that have been solved through the innovative use of what we now refer to as data analysis.

Problem 1: Retail

If retail businesses are able to determine which location they should ideally open an outlet at, this could lead to earning profits right from day one. Quite clearly, the datasets that they analyze involves who their customers are, where they live, and how much they generally spend. It can even extend to what these customers do at certain locations such as enjoying a cup of coffee or even shopping at a store for clothes.

Can you imagine what a retail outlet can do with this kind of information?

Data analytics is very customizable; much like a good tailor

Yes, higher profits. But this can also impact what and how many of these items have to be kept at that store since data analysis will tell you you which items your customers prefer purchasing. This can, in turn, impact efficiency, since you can allocate the minimum resources required to meet these needs.

Better still, when you collate information in such a manner, management also gets a decent overview of which products are most popular, and so, devote resources to producing those products.

Problem 2: Healthcare

Not only does data analysis help with discovering drugs but it also predicts disease progress in patients. On average, it takes twelve years for a drug to be officially submitted. In order to shorten, the use of certain algorithms help with determining the success of a drug depending on biological factors.

In fact, these data science and machine learning algorithms simulate how the body will react to different versions of the drug, which reduces time spent on lab experiments. The information from each simulation is in a continuous learning loop and helps predict the outcome of future experiments with a high level of accuracy.

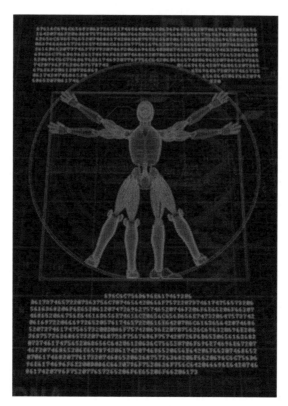

The Vitruvian Bot. Yes, machines can learn too!

When it comes to predicting disease progress, historical data about patients is collected and analyzed taking the necessary biomedical factors into account as well. Quite remarkably, doctors can take pre-emptive action and improve health outcomes for their patients. It's clearly a win-win, since it not only prevents the onset of disease but also reduces the amount of work that doctors have to do to arrive at such conclusions.

Problem 3: Finance

Financial firms like Amex not only predict loyalty based on analysing their customers' spending habit but they can also predict which customer accounts will close in a few months. It's amazing what analyzing trends can tell you about your own lives.

In addition to this, insurance companies are looking at data analytics to predict fraudulent claims before they occur. This is because it is an arduous process to detect which claims are fraudulent or not.

Banks have the ability to detect fraud through the power of data analytics

In using machine-learning algorithms that process large amounts of data to find these fraudulent cases, human auditors can then focus on only these cases and stop wasting time on ones that aren't. Not only can insurance firms prevent the loss of money from fraudulent claims but they can also reduce the number of man hours spent by their auditors to investigate fake claims.

When you see how far-reaching the effects of data analysis is, it should be clear that being comfortable with data is where our future lies. That said, let's understand a few key terms related to data that will serve as a foundation for conducting analysis as we move forward.

Defining Data

So, what is data? This is an apt question given how the focus on gathering, cleaning, and analyzing data has shaped into a science over the past decade or so. In the conventional sense of the word, data is nothing but factual information that can be captured or collected from a source.

On its own, this is broadly classified as raw data prior to being processed. However, when it is processed, by means of software such as SPSS, it transforms into information that helps tells a story. But there's more: this processed data can be considered as raw data for a series of other experiments, too.

Data when processed reveals trends

While this definition might seem a bit murky, it's best to consider an analogy that could help you understand it immediately. For example, take all the atoms in any substance or the cells in our body. That's what data amounts to when they stand on their own. The smallest unit of information that when collected and processed showcases a trend.

One must also note that 'datum' is nothing but a single data point that when accumulated over a period of time can be expressed as a single field of data. That said, when you accumulate several fields of data that are related - a customer's financial information is a common example - you get an entire dataset.

Now, while human-readable data consists of several types, there are two data types that are machine-friendly: numeric and non-numeric. These two types are also called qualitative and quantitative data, which is what we will define next.

Machine-Readable Data Types

There are two data types that machines can read and we will look at these two now.

Qualitative

Even if there's limited use for qualitative data in data analysis, it's still necessary to collect data that consists of text.

For example, you can understand the shopping habits of customers based on whether they're male or female. Let's say you run a store and make a list of all the customers who came in throughout the day until you closed up.

Guess who shops more? The clear winner!

You can easily tell what your customers' shopping preferences are based on their gender and whether more men or women visit your store regularly. All you have to do is record the gender of your customer and tally the number of men and women who visited your store separately.

There are a number of other reasons why qualitative data is collected, and for the most part work as categories of description themselves. Please keep in mind that qualitative data can be either nominal or ordinal depending on whether there exists an order or not. We will discuss this a little more later.

Quantitative

Now, quantitative data takes on the form of counts or measurements. In other words, this data type deals with numbers solely. While qualitative data, which is based on language, can vary according to one's experience, quantitative data is fixed. Further still, quantitative data can broken down into discrete and continuous values.

A simple example to explain this type of data could be the recorded number of sales made each day at the store or even the heights and weights of all employees in an office. That said, since the recorded number of sales will always be an integer, it is said to be a discrete value.

On the other hand, since the heights and weights of all employees can take any value and includes decimals, these values are considered to be continuous. There's a reason for this categorization and is what we will look at later.

Other

There's a third data type that does not classify either as qualitative or quantitative data but can serve as keys in cases. Take for example a car registration ID or an employee ID, which can be a sequence of just numbers or both numbers and alphabetical letters. It is not a measurement in the real sense, nor can one analyze this number. It does not classify as qualitative data since it cannot be segmented into ordered or unordered categories either.

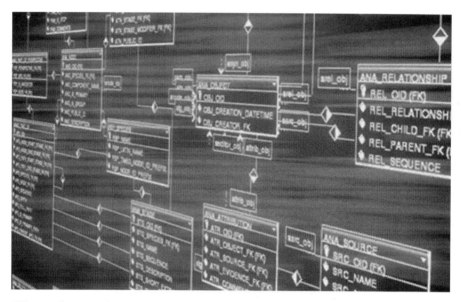

Where do you think you get good data from? Relational databases, of course!

However, much like a person's name in the real world, it uniquely identifies a single record of data consisting of values for all the variables in the dataset. Sometimes people in a single dataset can have the exact first and last names, so there is a need for this kind of data. A simple example of this would be one's employee ID that is linked to variables such as name, date of birth, weight, height, blood type, and current salary.

That said, it would be wise to remember that a single row of data in SPSS is called a 'case' while a single column is called a variable. This is no different from the information stored in databases, which are generally called records and fields.

Ordered & Unordered Data

There's another aspect of data that needs to covered and which can be broadly understood as ordered or unordered data. For the purpose of understanding this better, we have to remember what we read in the previous section about qualitative and quantitative data.

The only way we can carry out any statistical analysis on qualitative data is by obtaining its frequency. Statistical analysis deals largely with quantitative data and the measures that we arrive at in descriptive statistics.

One key difference between these two types of data is that we can rank quantitative data based on their measurements, while this isn't always possible or necessary with qualitative data. Having said that, let us look at the differences between nominal, ordinal, and scale or interval-based data.

Nominal

For example, if we wanted to count the number of apples, oranges, bananas, and watermelons bought at a store for the entire day and plotted it using a bar graph, you'd notice that there is no particular order that this list of items needs to be displayed.

Nor is there any numerical significance to any of these categories that you can use to rank this list of items either. In other words, you can count each of these items and list them in any order if you wish to. It really won't matter, because what you interpret from the graph will be the same. This type of data is called nominal data.

Ordinal *Likert*

The next type of data also includes the collection of qualitative data. However, there is one key difference with this type of data compared to nominal data. Referred to as ordinal data, this type generally occurs in customer feedback surveys that are ranked from angry to neutral to happy.

Of course, the highest rank is given to the happy category while the lowest rank is assigned to the angry category for obvious reasons. Assuming that the reader considers happiness to be the most positive experience, we enforce an artificial ranking here.

Still, there's another aspect of this type of data that differentiates it from scale or interval data. The only thing we cannot measure with this type of data is the true gap between happiness, neutrality, and anger unlike that of quantitative values. In other words, we know the gap between 5 and 10 is 5 units of measurement. This is not possible with ordinal data even if we assign an artificial ranking to each of the survey attributes.

Interval or Scale

Scale or interval data involves quantitative data, which bears the characteristics of having a specific order while also giving us a clear picture as to the numerical difference between two values based on the intervals in the scale.

For example, we know that temperature, whether Fahrenheit or Celsius, has specific intervals. Upon comparison of two values, we can tell the difference between 95 degrees and 105 degrees Fahrenheit, knowing that 105 degrees is higher in value.

These properties, as one can tell, cannot be found in both nominal and ordinal data. Best part: compared to the other two, we can carry the most number of statistical calculations with interval-based data.

While there is another type of data that involves ratios, we will not cover this topic as SPSS allows us to define our data using the characteristics of nominal, ordinal, and scale. We will cover this in the next chapter when we look at how we define our data in SPSS.

Is there a process for Data Analysis?

Yes. Data analysis is hardly the first step in this process. For the simple reason that there's no readymade data available. Not unless you have systems in place to capture various fields of data. Or you have created an experiment with tested methods for collecting data.

So, where does the process of data analysis begin? Where does it end? It definitely begins with data collection and ends with decision-making. Of course, one can also consider it to be ongoing, since our conclusions are continuously refined based on the inclusion of fresh datasets.

That said, here's the process of data analysis presented simply and adequately for any beginner:

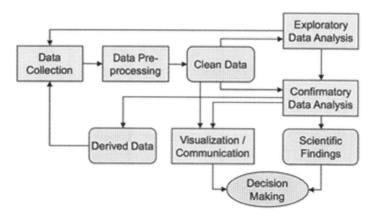

The Process of Data Analysis

A Note on Research Methods

Even if collecting data is not the focus of this book, it's still good to provide some background on methods used to collect either qualitative or quantitative data. This is also for the simple reason that SPSS was developed for the purpose of carrying out analysis for the social sciences. It helps to understand the various methods by which people collect both qualitative and quantitative data. Who knows? You might have to actually use one of these methods in the future.

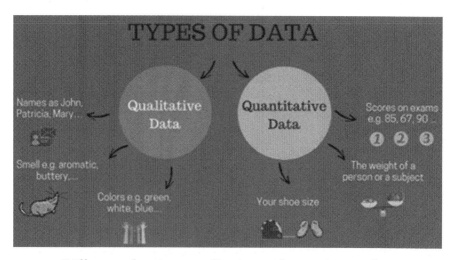

Difference between qualitative and quantitative data

Now, when we collect qualitative data, we are recording the experience, behaviour, and observations of participants associated with the study in terms of language. Sometimes, these observations can be our own as well. Since qualitative data is descriptive in nature, the methods that we use to collect data range from reading documents, diaries, and cultural records.

We can even look at physical artifacts to derive meaning or even conduct surveys and interviews with open-ended questions so as to gather qualitative data from participants. Of course, the immediate disadvantage is that we cannot analyze this type of data like quantitative data.

A simple ranked feedback survey can tell you a lot about your customers

Speaking of which, since quantitative data consists of numbers that can be categorized, ranked, or even serve as measurements, objectivity is achieved. However, unlike the methods used in qualitative research, the participants' responses are usually limited to a rating scale or simple yes and no questions as in polls and surveys.

However, the most popular means by which people collect quantitative data is by conducting natural, lab and field experiments. A traditional example of this is trying to determine the melting and boiling point of a substance.

Another example would be inpatient care where the nurse takes your pressure and temperature values to compare it against 'healthy' values.

Yet another example that can be added here are the content marketing metrics that Google records and uses to rank web pages in their search results page for certain keywords.

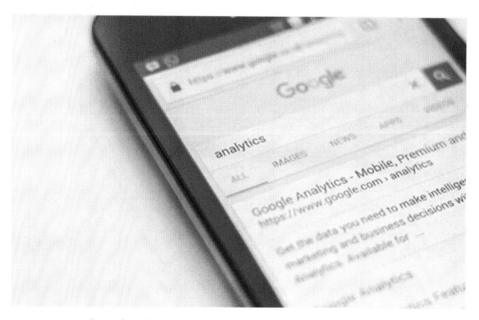

Google - I mean, Big Brother - is watching you!

As simple as these examples are, experimental design plays a big part in the values that are obtained as a result. We will look at this topic much later.

The Importance of Cleaning Data for Analysis

The importance of cleaning data prior to analysis cannot be understated. There would be no point analyzing the data if it fails to meets the required standards of quality. Apart from outdated observations, there are a few types of errors that we should look out for:

Duplicates

There's every chance that duplicate or irrelevant values tend to appear in datasets and one must be on the lookout for these errors. The reason why these data points must be removed is because, upon analyzing the data, this will lead to incorrect results and faulty conclusions.

Duplication of cases or records in SPSS - An Example

Structural Errors

This category of errors includes the incorrect entry of data at the time of measurement or even when the data is being transferred. As a result, you can have several variables that should be classified together but are now seperated. Mislabeling and typos can be reasons for these types of errors to occur. As one can expect, the results of your analysis will be poor, which is why keeping track of these errors and fixing them is vital.

Missing Data Points

This is a difficult type of error to deal with, as ignoring or eliminating the observation are not ideal actions here. Now, if you fill in the missing value based on similar observations in the dataset, this will not help as you are merely reinforcing a trend that was present already. Removing information is just as bad, since you are removing observations, you are reducing your chances of obtaining accurate information. Which is why it is advisable that one focuses on collecting all data points in observations as meticulously as possible.

Missing Data in the first cell under Maths

Errors in the form of Outliers

Outliers, by definition, are data points that lie well outside the range of values for any given variable. So, the question remains: should you remove it or keep these outliers? While some of these values might be authentic as part of a recorded observation, others might not. That said, if you find that some of the measurements recorded are not real values that can be produced in an experiment, it's advisable that you can remove the observation.

It should be obvious that the larger your dataset, the harder it might be to clean data. So, you should not rush the process of cleaning or preparing data for analysis. Ultimately using reliable data is the only way by which you can arrive at proper conclusions. There is no shortcut.

In the next chapter...

Now that we've gained an understanding of the nature of data in analysis, we move on to looking at what an SPSS data file is and what the layout of the SPSS Data Editor looks like. This is where we will also re-examine the concepts learned in this chapter, but in a hands-on way.

Chapter Four

The SPSS Data Editor

Much like audio, video, and documents have file extensions such as .mp3, mp4, and .docx, the extension for an SPSS data file is .sav. Just about everything you do henceforth will be saved in a data file. There are a couple of other types of files we will save when using SPSS such as an Output and Syntax file with extensions such as .sps and .spv, but this is for much later.

Opening a New Dataset in SPSS

As soon as you open SPSS, you have three options that involve either creating a new file or opening one that you've created earlier or exporting a file.

Since this is your first time using IBM SPSS, let's select New Dataset as highlighted in red below:

Open a New Dataset

Now, if you select New Dataset, you reach a spreadsheet-like screen that is titled Dataset1, as shown below:

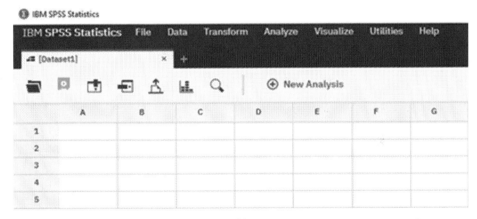

You can save this file as yourfilename.sav upon entering data

Since you have opened a new dataset, you will have to key in data in the rows and columns. As mentioned in the previous chapter, the columns are called Variables and the rows are called cases.

Entering Data in SPSS

Alright, now try entering some text and numbers in any of the cells available on the sheet. For example, enter your first name and the number 585. If you've worked with Microsoft Excel, this should be simple.

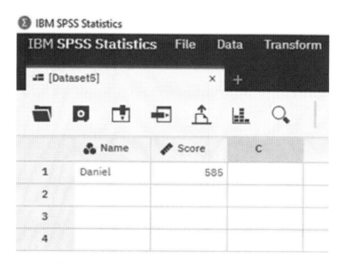

Enter your name and the number 585

The new version of SPSS is friendly to both numbers and text. It detects the type of data entered and alters the data type of the variable from quantitative to qualitative or vice-versa.

Still, you'll have to make a few more changes for that particular variable if you are entering data that has special characteristics. We'll deal with how you can do that shortly. Entering data is definitely important but learning how to define the variables as quantitative or qualitative data matters just as much in SPSS!

Version 25!

The Variable List in SPSS

Now, in SPSS version 25, this option of switching between the ...u and Variable view has been done away with. The new interface allows you to look at several details related to each variable by means of a pop-up menu while still being able to access your data.

Data or Variable View in Earlier SPSS versions

Having said that, look for Variable List at the bottom right-hand corner of your screen and as shown below:

Select Variable List to view the data types of six variables

Select the arrow highlighted in red in the Variable List tab which will throw up a list of characteristics that define each of your variables.

61

Select type of measure *

The Variable List in SPSS

Measure

We have three options under Measure, which are nominal, ordinal, and scale. Nominal can be selected if the values in this variable do not need to be categorized, as quantitative values usually are. For example, Name or Social Security numbers fall under this category.

 Ordinal, on the other hand, can be used to rank data, but where the quantitative difference between two data points is not fixed or known. For example, university grades or even satisfaction surveys that determine someone's happiness or unhappiness levels are nominal in nature.

The Scale option in SPSS is where you can both rank the data and where you already know the difference between the two quantities being compared. Time in seconds, hours, and minutes, temperature in Fahrenheit or Celsius, and Age in years come to mind as examples.

That said, select the correct measure for each of the variables from the drop-down list in SPSS v.25.

Name

The heading Name indicates the Variable Name that does not accommodate spaces between the labels not does it allow you to start the label with special characters or numbers. Just delete the term

name vs. label

VARIABLE001, VARIABLE002. VARIABLE003 and enter the desired name.

Label

This characteristic allows you to modify the variable name in the same way that you did for Name. When you open a new dataset, the variables will not be defined, as shown below:

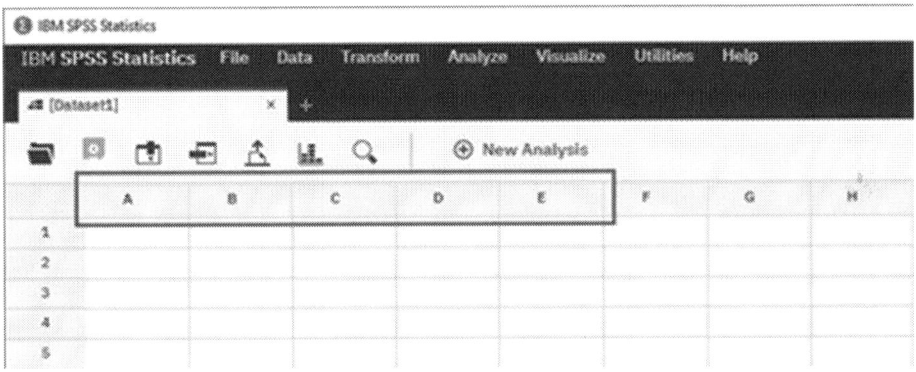

Empty Variable Labels

Once you make changes, as shown below under Label in the Variable List, the changes are automatically updated in the sheet:

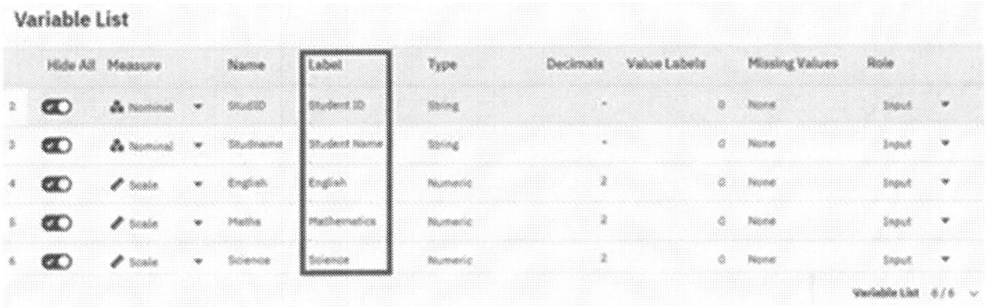

Update Variable List Label and check for changes in the sheet

As you can see below, the variable names in the image below now reflect the changes made in the earlier one:

63

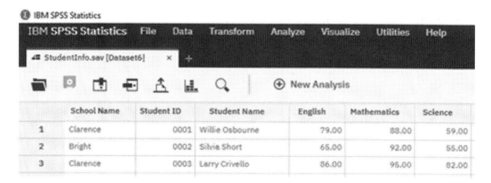

Updated Labels in Sheet

That said, the changes that you made in the Variable List for both Name and Label will be reflected here depending on whether you use either the Name or Label to identify your variable.

For this, you can find a toggle switch at the top right hand corner of your screen, and as shown below:

Use this to toggle between Variable Name and Label

Type

Now, you can change the variable type in Variable List by simply clicking on a particular variable at the point where its type is listed.

Point and click in the area circled in red to change the Data Type of Student Name

Make changes to the options as shown in the box that opens below. The options that open up in a drop-down list are Numeric, Comma, Dot, Scientific Notation, Date, Dollar, Custom Currency, String, and Restricted Numeric. Also, use the up and down arrows under width to increase the character width.

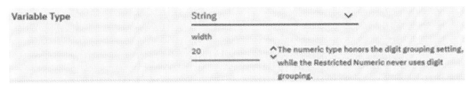

A width of 20 characters is permitted for String (or qualitative data) type

The options that open up in a drop-down list are Numeric, Comma, Dot, Scientific Notation, Date, Dollar, Custom Currency, String, and Restricted Numeric. Also, use the up and down arrows under width to increase the character width.

Decimals

If the type that you have selected is numeric, you can select the number of decimals that you would like to be displayed in the sheet. Simply, use the Backspace or Delete key to remove the current value and enter the number of preferred decimal places.

Value Labels

If you want to add names to certain values, then you would use this characteristic, but if not, just leave it as is.

Missing Values

By default, SPSS does not allow for values to be missing from a cell. In some cases, exceptions can be made. Since it's advisable to use data that is cleaned as much as possible, let's keep the default as is.

Role

Values under variable can take on the role of an input or target or output value. Or both. There's also the option of None that one can use to define the role of a set of values under said Variable.

Here are the options displayed in a drop-down list:

Select the role that the Variable should play

One last thing: if you cannot see the full Variable List properly, select the option below as circled in red in the top-right hand corner of the image:

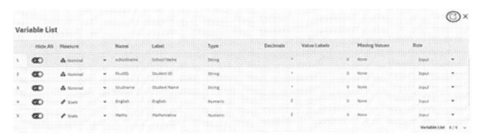

Selecting this option raises the Variable List to the top of the sheet for a full view

The Data Overview Pane

Now, if you want an overview of the data you have entered or exported into SPSS, you can select the Data Overview icon in the top right hand corner of your screen to open this pane:

Select this option to open the Data Overview Pane

Once you select this icon, you'll find that a pane opens up in the right hand side of your screen, as shown below:

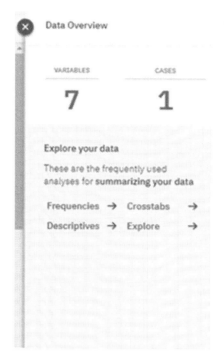

The Data Overview Pane

Not only does the Data Overview Pane account for the number of variables and cases, but it also gives you helpful pointers as to how you can summarize the data that you've keyed in or exported.

Just select any of the options highlighted in maroon in the figure above to do more with your data.

Open Multiple Tabs in SPSS

Now, every time you open an SPSS session and create a dataset, you are not limited to only conducting an analysis on that dataset. In other words, since SPSS v.25 offers the tabs feature, you can open several other datasets as well.

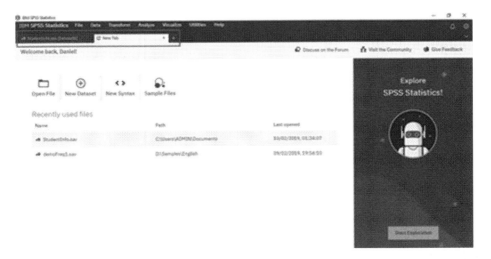

Multiple tabs in SPSS

For this, select the '+' sign next to the open tab in order to open a second tab. A new tab will open up as shown below and you can either choose to open a created dataset or populate data in a fresh, new one.

After this, you can switch between these tabs so as to look at both datasets simultaneously.

Search for Items

Now, there's another interesting option that is available in SPSS which involves conducting a quick search for items, be it Output, Dataset, or Syntax files. For this, click the arrow highlighted in red at the top right-hand corner of your screen:

Select the down arrow under the Settings cogwheel

Once you have selected this option, this drop-down box opens up below in which you can enter text in order to locate datasets, outputs, and syntax that you might have opened in several tabs.

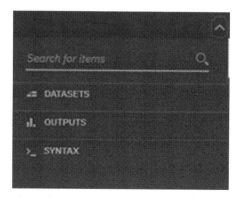

Enter a filename in the Search for Items textbox

This can prove to be especially handy if you have opened several datasets, outputs, and syntax, thanks to the new feature of being able to open several tabs in the SPSS Data Editor.

Settings & Notifications

Located at the top right-hand corner of your screen, you will find both the Settings and Notifications icons, as shown below:

Notifications [left] and Settings [right] icons

Select each of these icons in order to look at information pertaining to SPSS updates as well as to receive important notifications when complete running procedures, which we will look at later.

New Analysis

Now, once you've entered or exported all the data that you need for an analysis, you can conduct an analysis first by selecting a variety of options available once you click on New Analysis, as shown below:

Select New Analysis

Once you do, you are directed to another menu from which you can select an option for analysis amongst the several that are available. This Analyze Catalog section has several options. Pick one of them as shown below and begin with your analysis of data.

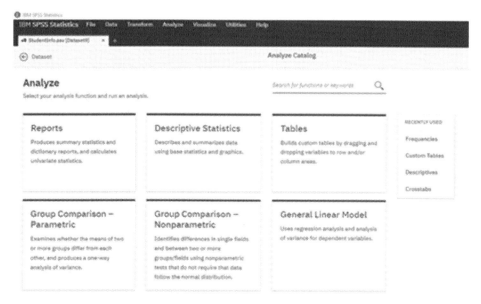

Analyze Catalog Menu

Other Useful Tab Functions

Now, there are a few other functions that you can run if you right-click on the tab of the current dataset you have opened. Let's look at what each of the options helps us with:

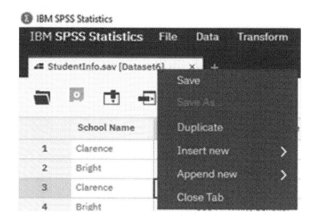

Right-click on the current tab

Save

Saves the current tab that you are working on.

Save As

Saves the current tab with a specific name.

Duplicate

Produces a duplicate of the tab.

Insert and Append New

Allows you to add a new dataset, output, or Syntax file.

Close Tab

Closes the current tab that you are working on.

In the next chapter...

Now, that we've covered the basic aspects of entering and defining data in SPSS, apart from familiarizing ourselves with the other features that help us work smarter in SPSS, let us now begin our exploration of Statistics right from the ground up.

Chapter Five

Introduction to Statistics

Even before we dive into the two main divisions of statistics as a study, it's good to question the need for a study in the first place. There's a lot of information around us today that comes in the form of statistics because this study has found its way into every facet of our lives.

If you like watching sports, the media almost always posts articles that ranks the highest-paid athletes in the world every other year. If you enjoy movies, you'll find articles that list the highest-paid actresses each year as well. An excellent example of this is Forbes, with its annual ranking of the richest men and women in the world.

While this information keeps us entertained, it merely keeps us in touch with what's happening in the world around us. But statistics can do a lot more for us apart from just keeping us informed with what and who matters in today's world.

The weather forecast... does it matter? Sure does

Politics and government, education, law enforcement, healthcare, technology, and businesses generate and analyze statistics to a great extent. Then there's advertising that tends to make bold claims about products and services. If that's not enough, the media tends to sensationalize findings just to get more attention with any social proof or conclusive data. This is where our ability to discern between what is true and false becomes important as a functioning member of society.

In stark contrast, there are a number of times when statistics have been used intelligently in order to make a difference in society. We must pay attention to such positives and applaud people for being conscientious and insightful through these efforts.

So, how do you do this? By developing statistical thinking on the whole and by being able to use its methods to question misleading statistics and bold claims that people make every other day.

To sum things up: at a basic level, increasing your knowledge about statistical methods makes it easier to distinguish between fake and real news. At the most, you could end up finding employment as a data scientist. A role that experts consider to be one of the hottest careers in the market today.

Data Science - so what do the numbers tell you?

Still, there's no doubt that you are going to use statistics for something or other in life, whether it involves buying goods or even a house, managing your budget, or even picking between two employers when looking for a new, better job.

Now that we've understood why a solid understanding of why statistics are necessary, let's continue this discussion by examining what statistical thinking truly entails.

A Definition of Statistics

The conventional definition of a statistic is that, as a number, it is a property or characteristic of that dataset. For example, the average annual salary at Microsoft could be a certain amount, and when you compare that value to the average salaries of people in similar positions at other technology firms, you can tell whether Microsoft pays its employees better or not. If you're applying for a job, using simple statistical calculations like this can improve our own lives.

Are you making enough? It's always worth checking

But before we dive into this simple process, one must keep in mind that there's a big difference between drawing conclusions from a data sample that has much fewer cases of data than the entire population. If anything, the more observations you can capture or record, the more accurate your conclusions.

Of course, this requires following a step-by-step process that begins with collecting to interpreting data in the final step. If we understand the process involved, we will truly understand what statistics are.

Step 1: Collect Good Data

As mentioned in an earlier chapter, if data is missing or inauthentic, the conclusions drawn from the statistical study conducted can be faulty.

While there are a range of methods by which you can collect qualitative and quantitative data, picking the most suitable method is worth considering based on the problem you'd like to solve.

There's a lot of factors at play in a study and the person who leads it must be sensitive to what works and what doesn't.

Step 2: Analyze Data

When it comes to analyzing the data, there are a number of methods used that help us draw conclusions from the data we have collected.

Probably the simplest of them that one can think of is counting; used during democratic elections, the counting of votes is where the winner is the one with the most.

It's easy. Just count the number of votes and you're done, right? There's much more.

Much more for a number of reasons!

In other studies, the performance of players in a team or students in a class can be calculated by determining the percentage of success or failure for a certain activity that they carry out.

Yet the question remains: how do these individual statistics calculated hold up against other students and players of sports teams? Better still, what can it tell us about the population as a whole?

On the whole, this is what makes the study of statistics so interesting because we can then begin to uncover why certain politicians, athletes, or students perform better than others. This, of course, depends on how we analyze the relationships between the variables in any of these studies.

Step 3: Visualize Data

Once we've completed analysis of the data, it's much easier to interpret the data if we can visualize it correctly. There are a number of visualizations available for this, such as histograms, box plots, pie charts, box plots, and scatter diagrams, and so on and so forth.

Knowing which visualization to use to present our findings can make all the difference since we ourselves, as humans, process visual information much better than in any other form.

Step 4: Interpret Data

This is the part where we begin to draw conclusions about the data we have obtained and. hopefully, take action for our own betterment. If we feel as if we are not earning much, conducting a simple analysis by collecting data from employees with similar responsibilities and years of experience across your industry can either lead you to change your job or stay put. Well, why not compare it against the entire population of employees too?

Going Late to Work - A Short, Statistical Study

Let's say you live in a city where traffic jams are common. Luckily, there are several routes to get to your place of employment. Keeping the phenomenon of being stuck in a traffic jam constant here, the shortest route to work isn't always the fastest way to get there.

Who likes traffic jams? Only people with nothing to do!

Of course, if your manager is one who wants his employees reporting to work on time, then you're in for a lot of trouble. Especially if you've been late to work due to these traffic jams. No matter what the excuse, you will be reprimanded for unprofessionalism for not being able to report to work at 9:00 AM sharp.

So, how do you resolve this issue using statistics?

For this, you can track the number of days you went to work on time and the days you did not. Of course, depending on the traffic, you would take different routes to work, which another variable that you should record as well. Time would be another variable that is worth considering here. This involves what time you left your place and how much time it took to get to work on time. You could even collect data on the type of transportation you used.

As shown in the table below, there are six cases recorded from six variables used to analyze the study:

	Date	Route Taken	Travel Time (in minutes)	Type of Transportation	Time You Left Home	Reached Office On Time
1	01/01/2019	Route 1	40	Taxi	7:30	Yes
2	01/02/2019	Route 2	45	Car	8:00	Yes
3	01/03/2019	Route 3	25	Bike	7:55	Yes
4	01/04/2019	Route 2	60	Bike	8:15	No
5	01/05/2019	Route 3	75	Taxi	8:20	No
6	01/06/2019	Route 1	65	Car	8:20	No

A Simple Dataset resolving the "Late to work" issue

While it's a good practice to collect as much authentic data for analysis, just looking at one's week's data can tell you enough if you want to report to work on time.

For starters, you can tell that the earlier you leave for work using any route or transportation method, the more likely you are to reach work on time. A simple count from the data above should tell you this. You can average the amount of time taken to reach work when you leave before 8:00 AM and compare it against the average amount of time taken to reach work when you leave after 8:00 AM. Of course, this might not always be possible, since there are times we wake up late or have chores to complete before leaving.

So, how do we make it on time, whether we leave early or not?

When one looks at the case where we use a bike as our mode of transportation, we find that it takes the least amount of time to reach work as a result. In stark contrast, taking a taxi or a four-wheeler after 8:00 AM regardless of route will mean that we will definitely be late.

We can also take note of the fact that taking Route 3 when running late is the best option.

As you collect more and more data, you can begin to check the impact of each of these variables on reporting late to work or not. Of course, when it comes to reaching conclusions or taking actions, if you cannot find a pattern that helps you reach work in the shortest time possible by the use of statistics here, then it's time to find another route to work or even decide that it is time to shift your place of residence closer.

Now, if you don't want to find another route to work or even shift your place of residence, that's where inferential statistics can play a role in telling how long it takes for you to reach work on certain routes when you take different modes of transportation. Based on which route you choose, the best mode of transportation and, hopefully, the ideal time after 8 AM that you can leave for work.

Having looked at a basic example and how we can use data to solve a simple problem, let's move on to understanding the two broad categories into which statistics are segregated.

Descriptive Statistics

If you've come across the terms mean, mode, median, variance, and distribution at some point in high school mathematics, you already have some idea as to what descriptive statistics consists of. But what do you use it for? How does it differ from inferential statistics? As useful as these methods of statistical analysis are, are there any limitations?

These are all excellent questions that are worth addressing one by one.

By definition, descriptive statistics summarize the data provided in a sample without drawing any conclusions or making any generalizations. For example, let's say that you want to look at how a class of 10 students performed in subjects such as Science, Mathematics, and English.

The Subject Average as a New Variable in SPSS

As the instructor, you might want to compare how the class has done overall from this dataset. If you derive the subject average earned by each by calculating the mean for each of the subjects, you are summarizing how each student has fared on the whole.

This is the purpose of descriptive statistics and, merely seeks to describe rather than glean any insights into how well the 10 students might have done compared to other batches of students or classes.

You can even see what the class average is for each student, as shown below:

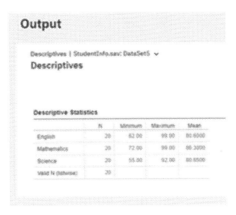

The Subject Average for English, Mathematics, and Science in SPSS

As you might have noticed, these students have fared better at Mathematics compared to the other two subjects here. But can you predict how they will fare in future tests? You can't. This is because descriptive statistics merely analyzes data that is available and cannot estimate what the average score for said subject is for all students studying in the same class across the city.

While this simple dataset is what is known as a sample, the population of the study could be all students studying in the same class in several schools in one city, state, or even the entire country. It really depends on what the researcher considers to be the population of the study itself.

Even if descriptive statistics seems limited, most statistical studies that are inferential in nature tend to use the results of an analysis generated from methods prescribed in descriptive statistics on a sample as a springboard to make inferences for the population on the whole.

That said, the focus of descriptive statistics is on central tendency, spread, and shape that a dataset takes on as a distribution of values which can represented by a number of visualizations, as mentioned in an earlier section. If you aren't sure what this means, please note that we will explore this topic in detail much later.

Inferential Statistics

Keeping in mind the difference between a sample and an entire population of data, there's one limitation that most statisticians are generally faced with: they cannot collect much less analyze data of an entire population.

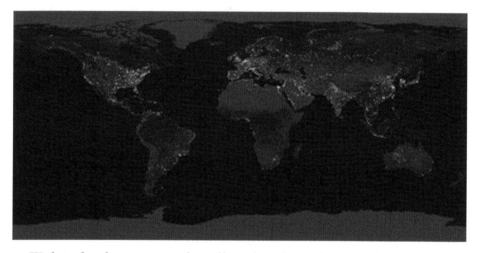

With technology, we might collect data from the global population soon

In other words, if we wanted to calculate the average that all students in a country obtain for English for a particular test that year, this is just not possible. So, researchers will often collect a much smaller sample of data and perform calculations to gain an understanding of how the students fared. But they go even further by using methods prescribed by inferential statistics to determine how students in a population could possibly fare in an English test.

This does not mean that the analysis performed on samples isn't applied to data that represents entire populations when possible. The only difference is that when you calculate the mean or standard deviation of a sample, this is a property of that particular sample of date. In the case of an entire population, its mean or standard deviation is commonly referred to as a parameter. It's important to note the difference between the two early in your understanding of statistics as a whole.

That said, in most studies, it is not feasible to collect data from the entire population to estimate these parameters. Moreover, common sense dictates that there's bound to be a sampling error if you average out the annual salaries of ten employees in a firm compared to an entire population of a million employees working across the country. Or for that matter, which Presidential candidate is going to win the elections?

So, faced with this obvious challenge, inferential statistics applies methods to estimate the parameters as well as test statistical hypotheses set by researchers in a study. We will look at inferential statistics in a future chapter.

In the next chapter...
Now, we will look at the functions in the SPSS drop-down menus. While this is merely an introduction to the functions that are available, try to remember where certain features are located so you know when to use them in the future. Please keep in mind that you do not have to use these features just yet. At least, not until we're done with a chapter on descriptive statistics.

Chapter Six

The SPSS Data Editor Menus

Given our introduction to statistics in the previous chapter, we will now take a look at the SPSS menus and the options that are available for the user. Now, remember that this chapter is also introductory in nature.

We will look at the SPSS menus that contain the functions that are necessary to carry out the statistical calculations that we will perform in the following chapters.

Please remember that even though we are not conducting any statistical analysis just yet, this chapter will help you remember key SPSS functions that you will need to use in the future.

So, without further ado, let us go through each of the menus that are located at the top left hand corner of your screen.

The File Menu

The first menu that we are going to look at is the File menu, which has eight functions that help you manage your datasets, Output, and Syntax files.

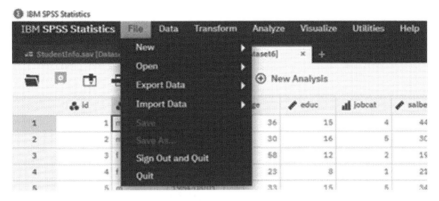

The File Menu

New & Open

When we point the mouse directly over New, we'll be able to open a new dataset, Syntax script, Output file, or a Python 2 or 3 script. This is no different with Open option as well.

Export & Import Data

As for the Export function, you should be able to export a dataset created in SPSS as a .csv file. The Import function allows you to populate data into new SPSS dataset from both .csv and Excel files.

Save & Save As

The Save and Save As allows you to save both a newly created dataset and Syntax script as a .spv and .sps file.

Sign Out & Quit and Quit

Finally, the Sign Out and Quit option allows you to sign out of your IBM id entered when you first installed SPSS and quit. If you don't have a strong reason to do so, then it is preferable to use the Quit option instead.

The Data Menu

As one can tell, the Data menu deals with a number of functions that involve manipulating data that are found in variables and cases. So, let us examine some of these that you will use most commonly:

Identify Duplicate Cases

This function helps us to find cases that are repeated. As we discussed earlier, missing or duplicate cases can mean that the analysis we carry out will not produce accurate results.

The Data Menu

Identify Unusual Cases

This function helps you to identify cases that are unusual within a range of values. Otherwise known as outliers, these numeric values lie outside the range of the data we are looking at. In the case of qualitative data, it looks for entries that are different from the others. This function is very useful because it allows you to detect incorrect data, whether missing or otherwise.

Select Cases

Now, if you are looking for a range of numeric or non-numeric values in the dataset under a particular variable, you can use this function to find these values. Of course, you have to specify certain conditions using operators to sift through the data.

Sort Cases

Now, you can sort cases based on the values in a particular variable whether numeric or non-numeric. By default, this options helps you do this in the Ascending Order.

Sort Variables

Using this option, you can rearrange the variables in any dataset either by Measure, Label, Name, Type, Decimals, and Values. If you remember, these are the very characteristics by which you defined your variables at the beginning.

Merge File

If you want to combine one dataset with the current one you are working with, then you can select Merge File option.

Split File

You can use this function to split the file into groups of cases that you can analyze further. Let's say you have a dataset containing students from two schools. You can split the dataset into two by sorting out the student data based on which school they attend.

The Transform Menu

While the Data Menu helps with the variables and cases but not directly manipulating the data itself, the Transform Menu helps us do much more with the data we have. Let us look at some of the common functions used from this menu:

Compute Variable

This function helps us compute new variables from existing ones. For example, if you need to find the average student performance in a dataset, you can use the functions provided when you select this function to do so. The data that you obtain upon computation will be added to a new variable.

Shift Values

This function helps you move an entire variable for whatever purpose. At first glance, this function seems like a method by which you can copy the data of a an entire variable elsewhere.

Recode into Same Variables

If for some reason you want to use numbers to represent qualitative data, you can use this function to recode the data from non-numeric to numeric data. As soon as you are done applying changes, the data in the variable selected will change in the data editor immediately.

For this very reason, it isn't safe to use this function, not unless you are very sure. One reason for this is because you cannot easily undo the changes made, which can cause you to lose the data entered for that particular variable.

Recode into Different Variables

Much like the previous function, this one helps you to recode the data in a variable. However, the difference is that it gets populated into another variable instead of changing the data in the variable that has been chosen for recoding.

Replace Missing Values

This function helps you add missing values in any variable to ensure that you have populated all data points. While it isn't good to have missing data points, sometimes you will just have to use this function.

The Analyze Menu

The Analyze Menu is an important one for the beginner, intermediate, and expert SPSS user. There are a number of options available in this menu that cater to the kind of data analysis that you are trying to carry out, ranging from descriptive to inferential statistics.

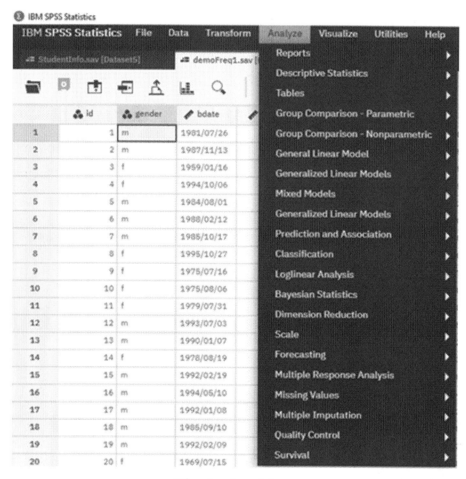

The Analyze Menu

While it might not be possible to run tests for every single option on this list, you will be able to understand what these functions will do as we cover options in statistical theory as simply as possible.

The Visualize Menu

As you can see, the Visualize Menu has only one option: Chart Builder.

The Visualize Menu

As obvious as Chart Builder is, you can plot several types of graphs depending on the variables and values in your dataset.

You can find a list of the chart types as soon as you select the Chart Builder option, as shown below:

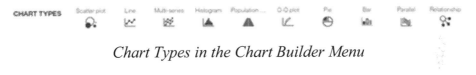

Chart Types in the Chart Builder Menu

We will build some of these charts in the future, so we will visit this menu in future chapters.

The Utilities Menu

The Analyze Menu is the second-last menu that we will cover in this chapter and that has a few extended features that one can use if they want to automate their tasks.

The Utilities Menu

Run Script

As discussed earlier, we can open Python 2 and 3 scripts for SPSS in the New and Open options under File. The Run Script feature helps you to run those very scripts that you've loaded.

Production Facility

Based on how quickly you learn how to use SPSS, there will come a point when you will need to run the same analysis repeatedly. While this can be boring, being able to automate and run certain analyses like this can help you get on with other tasks in the meanwhile. One example of this is generating weekly reports. Now, when you use this feature, you can continue working on an analysis while this job runs in the background. Of course, you can schedule it to run at a specified time as well.

The Help Menu

The Help Menu is the last menu that we will cover in this chapter and that has a lot to do with getting more information on how to use SPSS or to make it much easier. It's a sharp learning curve when navigating through SPSS for the first time, which is why it is necessary to access Help topics regularly.

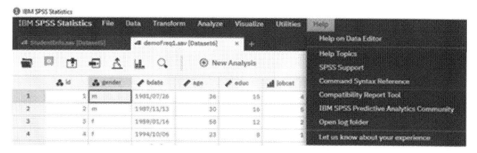

The Help Menu

Help on Data Editor

Selecting this option takes you to SPSS help files available over the internet and to a specific page based on the last action you took when using the Data Editor. For example, if you were trying to schedule a

Production Job under Utilities, selecting this option will take you to the help file for this option.

Help Topics

Selecting this option takes you to the main page where you have access to Tutorials, Case Studies, and Reference for Command Syntax, and so on and so forth.

SPSS Support

Selecting this option takes you to the IBM Developer Page where you can get information about licensing and other SPSS-related queries. Since there are a number of features that comes with software packages, people are going to get stuck if they're trying to perform complex statistical analysis. SPSS Support can help you with that.

Command Syntax Reference

As mentioned earlier, you can automate your analysis by using SPSS Syntax. As a beginner, you will mostly use the menus, but over time, you can invoke Syntax commands to run analyses over and over again. When you select this option in the Help menu, you'll be directed to a Help page online that lists all Syntax commands used.

Compatibility Report Tool

Now, this option helps you find information about the operating systems that support a particular product. You are directed to a page that helps you locate information concerning any IBM related software that you might be interested to use for your business.

IBM SPSS Predictive Analytics Community

Since the creators of SPSS literally brought the field of Predictive Analytics to life, there's an entire community at your disposal to help you with your data analysis tasks. Not only can you read the official SPSS blog but you can get answers and download extensions from the page you are directed to when you select this option in the Help Menu.

Open log folder

As expected, when you select this option, you'll be directed to a folder that will give you access to the log files that contain information when you are either installing or working with SPSS. These files are very useful if you are troubleshooting for issues. Since it requires technical knowledge, this option is usually for system administrators or developers to access and solve any issues with your installation of SPSS.

Let Us Know About Your Experience

As the last option in the Help menu, you get a chance to share your experience about SPSS via a feedback survey. Not only will you have to furnish information about your job role, organisation, and operating system, but you can tell them how satisfied you were when it came to using a number of SPSS features.

Quick Access to Important Functions

Now there are a few functions that are displayed in a toolbar format that can be accessed quickly that are highlighted in red in the figure above. Let us look at each of these functions from left to right.

Key Functions in a Toolbar Format

Open Dataset

As is evident, you can open a second dataset with this option. Or open the first one, if you haven't opened one already. As we learned in a previous chapter, the opened dataset can be accessed in a second tab.

Save As

Much like the Save As option in the File menu, you can save a new dataset by selecting this function.

Insert Variable

You can insert a new Variable using this option but first you need to select a cell in the right column when you'd like to enter your values.

Insert Case

You can insert a new case using this option but make sure you select a cell in the right row to enter your values.

Export

Much like the Export Data option in the File Menu, you can export a dataset in the .csv format when you select this option.

Chart Builder

Similar to the Chart Builder function in the Visualize Menu, you can select this option to build a chart of your choosing.

Find and Replace

You can locate data in any cell using this option. This will really come in handy if you have several variables and cases to go through.

Other Case and Variable Menu Functionality

Now, when you right-click in the datasheet area or any of the case numbers, you'll find a menu that involves manipulating cases opens up.

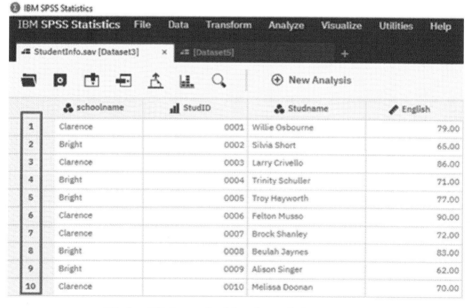

Right-Click on the Numbered Cases area

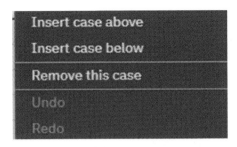

Select any option in this menu to edit your cases

Here's a summary of what these actions related to cases can help you with:

Insert Case Above

Selecting this option helps you insert a single case above the currently selected highlighted cell.

Insert Case Below

Selecting this option helps you insert a single case below the currently selected highlighted cell.

Remove this case

As evident, this option removes a single case but you have to highlight a cell in that case. You can also select multiple cell in consecutive cases and remove them as a result.

Undo & Redo

Most computer users would be familiar with these two options. The first allows you to undo the previous action while the latter repeats the action.

As shown below, we can access another menu that will be displayed when you right-click in the area where the variable names are located:

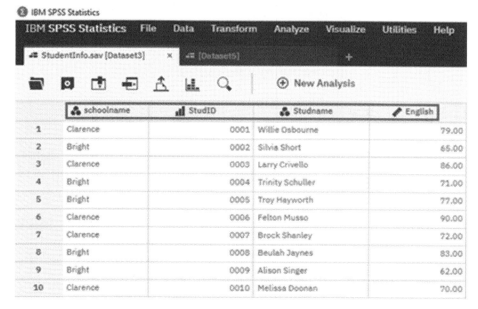

Right-click on any of the Variable Names

Also, another menu opens up with the following options and we will only cover a few basic ones for now:

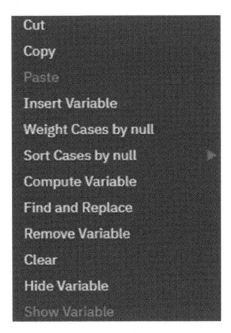

Some Variable Menu options are available in other menus too

As you can see, all these functions or option pertain to the editing of variables. Let's look at what some of these options offer, in terms of functionality:

Cut, Copy & Paste

As ubiquitous as these actions are, these allow you cut, copy, and paste data in a single variable or several of them.

While cutting or copying is simple, the paste function is a bit more complex. To paste data into a new variable, look for the three maroon dots lined up vertically on that Variable label and select that drop-down menu.

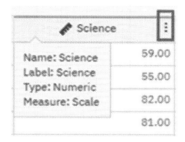

Select this menu to paste Variable data

When you complete this action, you should find the drop-down menu as shown below:

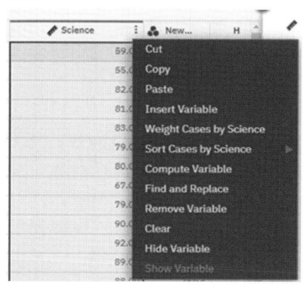

Select Paste in the menu in order to add the selected contents

Select Paste and enter the data that you have either cut or copied from another variable.

Insert Variable

This option allows you to insert a variable.

Compute Variable

This option allows you to add a new variable with data that has been computed be arithmetic, trigonometric, or even statistical in nature.

Find & Replace

Use this option to find a data point and replace with the right data.

Remove Variable

You can use this option to delete an entire variable.

Clear

Use this option to clear out the data from a selected variable.

Hide & Show Variable

You have the capability of hiding a single variable of data. After which, you can show the variable by opening the above drop-down menu again.

In the next chapter...

Now that we've explored the various SPSS menus and their functions, let us switch to continuing our theoretical discussion of descriptive statistics in the next chapter.

Chapter Seven

Descriptive Statistics

As mentioned in an earlier chapter, descriptive statistics are everywhere. We read it in the newspapers, blogs, textbooks, and even see them when watching television. While several fields of data belonging to a group of movie stars or football players might tell you nothing, descriptive statistics comes to the rescue for that very reason.

Descriptive statistics helps you find averages or means

In other words, when you run an analysis of any dataset using the methods prescribed in descriptive statistics, they reveal several insights about this dataset than you wouldn't be able to decipher otherwise. It's even better if you have more data from the past that serves as context and can help one compare these two datasets to detect a positive or negative trend.

Of course, just saying this would mean nothing without concrete examples, where data analysis uses descriptive statistics.

Common Applications of Descriptive Statistics

Here are some of the common situations in which descriptive statistics have proven to be useful:

1: Since a company like Google or Microsoft has to release quarterly reports of profit or loss generated, a number of the statistics developed in these reports are generally descriptive in nature.

2: School or university management would want to know how their students are doing each year at the subjects that they take. Of course, the summaries of the data that they collect is generally compared to data obtained from other schools. One of the simplest ways in which descriptive statistics are used at the end of the year is when we rank students according to their grades or marks and where the top-scoring students make it to a special list. The higher your CGPA, the better off you are in school.

Remember how much fun tests were to take in high school?

3: During election time, people might want to know which candidate might win the election based on historical data. This kind of data analysis is conducted in great depth as a way to predict who might win the election. Of course, collecting data for such a difficult analysis has to be sampled, but descriptive statistics are still used here.

4: Another popular use of descriptive statistics these days involves the evaluation of one's online marketing efforts.

5: This list would not be complete without those bloggers who make ranking lists about the highest paid movie stars, footballers, and tech CEOs, and so on and so forth today.

With that said, let's examine the dataset once again, but in the light of descriptive statistics.

Examining Datasets and their Distribution

As defined earlier, a cleaned dataset consists of variables and cases with data points that are authentic and valid. Just about any dataset will contain a list of values that fall within a range with the exception of a few values.

When we create a chart mapping these values, we get what is commonly known as a bell-shaped curve. This is where half the values are located in the left part of the curve and the other half is located to the right. Also, one can see that most of the values tend to be grouped close to the center when we visualize the values in the dataset by using a graph.

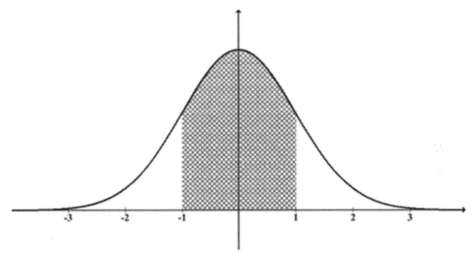

The bell shaped curve

Such distributions are said to be symmetric due to the shape of the bell-shaped curve that has been formed, thanks to a spread of the values that favour aggregation at the center.

Why should we know this?

Most datasets whose observations that have been derived from nature tend to follow this bell-shaped curve. That said, not all datasets when plotted will display this distribution, but it is still important to understand what a normal or symmetric distribution is in relation to any dataset of values that you might use for analysis.

Even if this topic is generally brought up when students study topics such as probability and random variables; being able to visualize your dataset of values as a distribution of values can set the stage for the measurements that we attempt to carry out in descriptive and inferential statistics.

Keep this bell shaped curve in mind as we begin to discuss the measurements of central tendency, spread, and shape in the following sections.

What Do Descriptive Statistics Measure?

Now, there are three broad aspects that descriptive statistics attempts to measure: central tendency, spread and, shape. All of the measures described under these three aspects contribute to being able to make accurate predictions from a sample of data. But for now, let us define and understand how we calculate each of these statistics with any given set of values in a dataset.

Measures of Central Tendency

The term 'Central Tendency' can be simply understood as the likelihood for values in a dataset to be located as close as possible towards the center. Now, there are three measures that fall under this category:

Mean

Also known as the average of values, we obtain this statistic by dividing the sum of all the values by the number of values for a single variable.

A simple example should explain how we calculate the mean here, if one isn't familiar with the procedure already.

The first measure of central tendency

Let's say we have a variable consisting of 5 values namely 10, 12, 8, 16, and 6. When we sum up the values we get a total of 52.

According to the formula, we have to divide 52 by 5 and obtain a mean of 10.4.

Simple, yes?

So, let's move on to the next measure of central tendency.

Median

By definition, the median is the value that is located at the center of a set of values and which is identified once the set is ordered in ascending order.

Yes, something like this median!

For example, let's look at the same list of five values we used to calculate the mean which is 10, 12, 8, 16, 6.

When we rearrange the values in ascending order, we get: 6, 8, 10, 12, 16.

As is evident, the third value in the set is center-most value. So, the median for this set of values is 10.

Now, when we have even number of values in a set such as 6,6,8,9,10,11, we pick the two middle values and find the average. In this case, 8+9/2 will give us 8.5. This is the median of the set.

One good reason why this measure is used sometimes is because it can still give us a good idea of the location of the center value despite having a number of values that are too high or low.

Mode

This measure tells us which value occurs the most in a set of values. For example, if our dataset consists of ten scores of students in an English test such as 90, 89, 97, 84, 90, 69, 73, 90, 99, 90.

So, which English score was most common here? 90, as you can see.

Learning to count has always been a part of mathematics

For this simple example, the mode is considered to be 90 even if there are times when you can get two numbers that occur the most number of times. Still, calculating the mode can be useful when we have categorical data as part of our dataset.

With that said, we have looked at the three measures of central tendency and will now move to a less common measure that one might have come across in descriptive statistics.

Measures of Spread

While the measures of central tendency finds the middle value or average of a set of values, the measures of spread tends to the look at the distribution of values from the lowest value to the highest value of the set. This important measurement called variance defines how close or far apart all the values in a set are from each other.

Minimum, Maximum & Range

This measure is easy to calculate. We find the maximum and the minimum value in the set and find the difference.

For example, if we take this set of 5 values consisting of 6, 8, 10, 12, 16, 6 is the minimum value while 16 is the maximum value.

Hence, when we find the difference between the two, we obtain the value 10. This is the range of the entire set of values.

InterQuartile Range

The term 'quartile' is defined as one of the four equal parts that a set of values can be divided into. The values of these quartiles is the middle value or median from each of these parts and is usually referred to as Q1, Q2, and Q3.

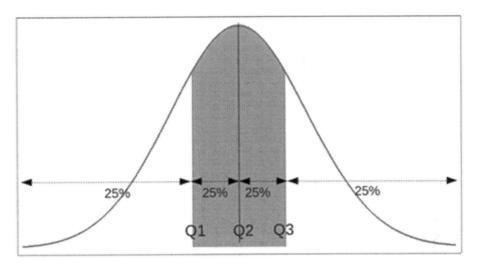

Quartiles, as depicted visually

Let's take a set of 10 values such as 30, 32, 32, 35, 38, 42, 46, 48, 50, 50.

From prior learning, what would be the median here? We can calculate this to be 38+42/2, which equals 40.

Now, that we've calculated the median of the set or Q2, it is time to find the middle values of the other two quartiles where Q1 consists of the values 30, 32, 32, 35, while Q3 consists of values such as 46, 48, 50, 50.

We find the median of the Q1 quartile by finding the median, where 32+32/2 gives 32. So, the value of Q1 is 32. Finally, we calculate the value of Q3 by finding the median of the upper quartile, where 48+50/2 results in the median being 49.

Having said that, since the formula for finding the Interquartile Range is Q3-Q1, we perform the following calculation: 49-32 = 17.

Based on the bell curve theory that we looked at first, a majority of values in a dataset is said to lie in the middle. So, when we calculate the Interquartile Range, we can see where most of our values lie.

But why do we calculate the IQR? First, we are able to see the spread of values in the dataset. Importantly, we will also be able to identify outliers in the set. These are values that are distant from most of the other values in the set.

How we do this is by determining the range of the set by using two formulas. For the lower limit, we use the formula, Q1 - 1.5 * IQR. The upper limit is determined by the formula, Q3+1.5*IQR. Any values in the set that lie outside these limits are known as outliers.

Variance

To calculate variance, we first find the difference between each value in the set and the arithmetic mean, which is squared to compensate for negative and positive differences. After this, we obtain the sum of the squared values and divide it by the number of data values minus one in the set.

Let us demonstrate this with an example. Consider the set with four numbers 1,2,3,4. The arithmetic mean of this set is 2.5. In order to calculate variance in this set, this is what we do:

Step 1: $(1-2.5)^2 + (2-2.5)^2 + (3-2.5)^2 + (4-2.5)^2$ divided by 4

Step 2: 2.25 + 0.25 + 0.25 + 2.25 divided by 4

Step 3: 5 divided by 3

Your variance after completing this calculation is 1.67.

Standard Deviation

One might wonder if we calculate variance, why do we need the standard deviation measurement at all? After all, standard deviation is just the square root of the variance that we just calculated.

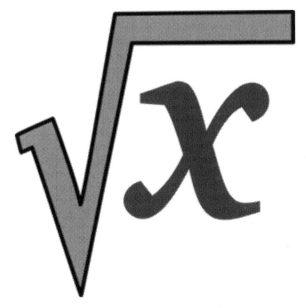

Where x is the variance calculated

In the example above, that amounts to 1.29. So, why do we need this value?

Unfortunately, as we had to square the difference between each of the values from the mean, the final value we end up with is not the same as the original unit of measurement. In other words, if our set consisted of values measured in centimeters, the variance would take on the unit of centimeter squared. This is because 5 cm into 5 cm gives us 25 centimeters squared. Our new value is not length but has been converted into a unit of area.

In order to reduce it to the original unit of measurement, we find the square root of variance, which is what we call standard deviation.

Having said that, when one obtains a high standard deviation value, it means that the values in the set are spread out over a wide range and vice-versa.

Having looked at these two important measures in descriptive statistics, let us look at the final measure, and that is the shape of the distribution of values.

Measures of Shape

When looking at this aspect of descriptive statistics, we are mostly concerned with whether our observed values take the shape of a normal or skewed distribution.

Since we already mentioned earlier that normal distributions are also symmetrical, skewed distributions would point to the fact that the observed values that we have used in our analysis leads to an asymmetrical distribution.

In the case of a normal distribution, we know that it follows the 3-sigma rule. However, not all distributions are shaped this way, which is where two measures come in: skewness and kurtosis.

Skewness

The skewness of a distribution is calculated by finding out how centered the mean of the distribution is in relation to its values. It helps in being able to determine which measure of central tendency is most applicable to the dataset in question. A normal distribution is said to have a measure of zero skewness.

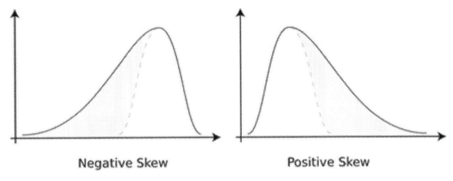

Negative Skew   Positive Skew

Yes, there exists a measure for skewness

In other cases, if most of the values are concentrated to the right while the tail to the left is longer, the distribution is said to be negatively skewed. When the majority of the values are concentrated to the left with a long right tail, it is said to be positively skewed. Another way to determine whether it is positively or negatively skewed is to look at the mean, median, and mode values. In the case of the former, the mean and median will be smaller in value than the mode, while in the latter, their values will be smaller. A distribution with no skewness will have identical mean, median, and mode values.

We can calculate skewness by using the formula that uses the number of values in a set, the standard deviation of the distribution, as well as the cube of the sum of the difference between each of the values and their arithmetic mean.

Seem complicated? Don't worry. SPSS will calculate this for you anyway, which is what we will look at in the next chapter.

Kurtosis

Kurtosis is another measure of shape that deals with the tails of a distribution. If you remember the Normal distribution that we first looked at, both lines that seem to meet the x-axis at a given point are said to be the distribution's tails.

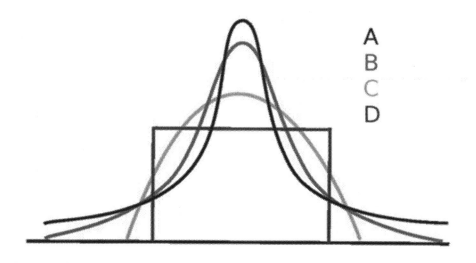

How each of the tails are shaped tell a story

While skewness helps us determine which measure of central tendency is most appropriate, kurtosis looks at the outliers in the distribution. If there are more outliers, the tails of the distribution will be much longer. If there are very few, then the distribution in question is as normal as it can get.

Statisticians look for high or low kurtosis to determine whether they have too many outliers in the set of data itself. In other words, there might be something wrong with the way they collect observations.

Obviously, this means that they have to repeat the process again or eliminate the unwanted outliers from the dataset itself.

The Importance of Using Charts

Let's admit it: we love visual content much more than textual. At least, most of us do. In fact, even before we have processed this information, we show interested in visual information because it is appealing to the eye as well.

Based on finding from a number of studies, it takes our brain about a quarter of a second to process the visual information that we take in. This is not so with text. In other words, it's easier. This type of communication really helps, since attention spans have dropped to almost 8 seconds today.

Albert Bierstadt's artwork on Nature... worth more than a million words?

That said, if it is easier to process and interpret visual information, we find it much easier to retain that information as well. In fact, we are hardwired to process information this way, and so it only makes sense that the world, with new digital technologies at our disposal, use it to great effect to convert textual or numeric information into informative, attractive visuals.

Quite clearly, this study on visuals works in tandem with using charts for descriptive statistics. Even if the focus isn't on making this form of visual information attractive, any chart that we use must be both clear and readable. Or else, the purpose would be defeated.

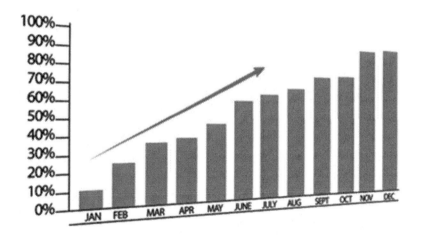

Clear and readable?

There's another reason why using charts help. Let's say that data is complex to understand merely in terms of numbers or text. A visual representation can help us gain insights if there exists a relationship between two variables or we are able to see a trend. In other words, if a chart helps us grasp information clearly, then it would be wise to use it. Or else, it wouldn't be necessary at all, now would there?

Another aspect to consider would be using the right kind of chart to display information that would be insightful to the viewer. There are a number of types of charts that are used for specific types of experiments, which is something that is worth considering given the dependent and independent variables that you have collected data for in said experiment.

Lastly, there are a few errors that one must keep in mind when creating a chart. Duplicate data is a no-no while the lack of legends and labels can cause the reader to misinterpret what you're trying to convey. Still, most of these errors can be done away with when using SPSS, as the chart that you create requires detailed information.

Since preparing charts goes hand-in-hand with descriptive statistics, we will now look at the most common types of graphs that are available for different sets of data.

Presenting Descriptive Statistics Using Charts & Graphs

As mentioned earlier, each of these types of charts can be used effectively depending on the type of data you've collected in your experiment. In order to be able to use charts well in SPSS, let's take a closer look at the common types of charts that are used in Descriptive Statistics:

Line & Multi-Series Charts

These were the most common charts used when we were in school, weren't they? You have the X and the Y axis where you would plot the data points for the independent variable in the X-axis and the dependent variable in the Y-axis.

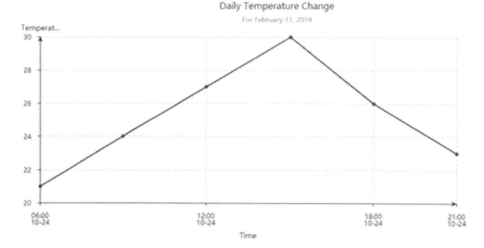

Can you see how the temperature changes every 3 hours?

So, what does the line chart do? In this example, one can see that we really gain speed in the fourth second compared to the speed in the third second.

In other words, this means that we can compare the changes in speed with the passing of each time interval here. For anyone who lives in a city with such temperature changes, you'd know how hot or cold it is during any time of the day or night, provided you have analyzed large amounts of data.

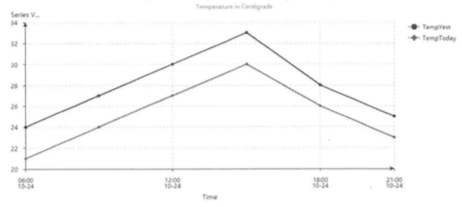

Comparison of Temperatures on a Multi-Line Graph

You can clearly tell that the average temperature of Sunday was much lower than Saturday. As you see this trend over several Sundays, you'd know that this day is an excellent day to be out and about. You can analyze temperature trends for each day of the week for several months and arrive at which day is the coolest from the data you analyze.

Pie Charts

This is another common chart that is used when you want to group qualitative data in a way that yields quantitative results. Since cake is usually sliced into big and small pieces and gives us a visual sense of proportion, one can easily do the same when using a pie chart. Let's say you wanted to find out the break-up of young, middle-aged, or elderly customers who visit your online store each day.

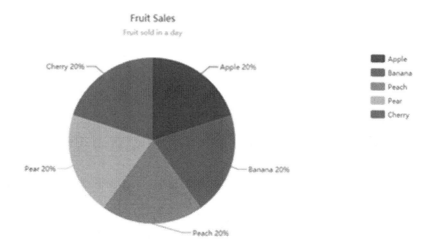

Fruit Sales represented on a Pie Chart

Of course, you can collect entire sets of data like this over months and begin to cater to customers of a specific age group by showcasing products that they like best.

Histograms & Bar Charts

While a histogram represents the frequency of numerical data which is continuous, bar graphs represent the frequency of qualitative data.

However, the difference between the two is that the former displays the data using continuous numerical intervals as bins while the latter does not.

Let's look at the difference between a histogram and a bar charts using two different sets of data.

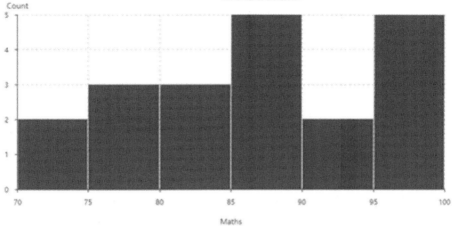

Mathematics Scores Overview

For the histogram, we want to see how many students earned scores between 50 to 100 in Mathematics. For the bar charts, let us see how many people you know watch different sports.

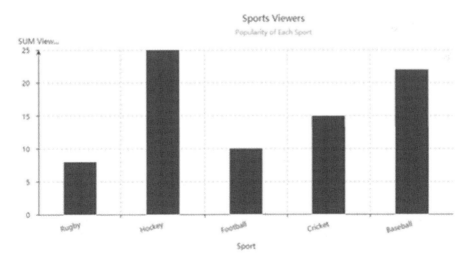

Bar Chart for Sports Viewers

If you look at X-axis label for the Sports Viewers Bar chart, you will find that it is a categorical variable. On the other hand, the X-axis label for the Mathematics score histogram is a numeric variable where continuous intervals serve as bins to count the different values.

Box Plot

As you wrap your head around the idea of how data forms a normal distribution, the box plot is another graphing method that can reveal the distribution of values for said dataset. While the measures of central tendency are but few, finding the spread of these values matters just as much.

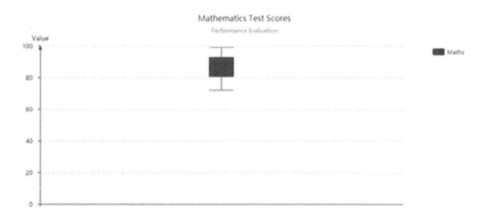

Boxplot for Mathematics Test Scores

Having said that, using the box plot will not only give you the median but will provide visual information about the interquartile range, whiskers, outliers, and the minimum and maximum values of the distribution.

As a result of this information, you will also be able to find out if the distribution is skewed or not or whether the range of values in the distribution meets conditions for a symmetrical distribution.

Scatter Plot

Last but not the least, we look at the scatter plot that also plots variables similarly to the line chart where the independent variable is usually across the x-axis and the dependent variable is plotted along the y-axis.

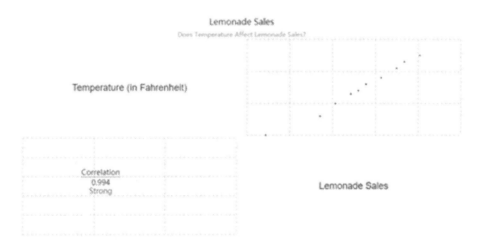

Lemonade Sales using a Scatter Plot

The scatter plot is used when you are trying to find a correlation between these two variables of data and you would like to generate a line of best fit or a trend line. For this you will have draw a line that is as close as possible to all points.

Doing so successfully will result in the activity where you can obtain values from carrying out interpolation and extrapolation so as to obtain conclusions from the overall dataset. One must be careful with extrapolation as this involves determining values that are outside the range of the dataset in use.

In the next chapter...

We will look at the steps involved in calculating each of the measures we discussed in descriptive statistics for central tendency, spread, and shape in SPSS. In other words, we will now apply the theory learned in this chapter by conducting data analyses on a variety of created datasets.

Chapter Eight

Computing Descriptive Statistics using SPSS

Following our understanding of descriptive statistics and graphs in the last two chapters, it's time to put it all together by carrying out data analysis to find the measures of central tendency, spread, and shape.

Even though we have looked at how these measures are calculated, you really won't need to do this given that SPSS calculates everything for you and does much more. It's still good to know a bit of theory so that we can use these measures far more effectively.

Now, depending on the data you are analyzing, you can calculate each of the measures in descriptive statistics in SPSS and generate a chart along with it. Still, since it might seem a bit confusing when it comes to using the software package, let's learn how to calculate each of these statistics learned one by one.

For starters, let's learn how to use the Frequency function in SPSS to count the number of Computer Science students belonging to three different universities from a dataset of 6 variables and 20 cases.

·equency

Once you have your dataset opened in SPSS, open the Analyze menu, select Descriptive Statistics, and then select Frequencies.

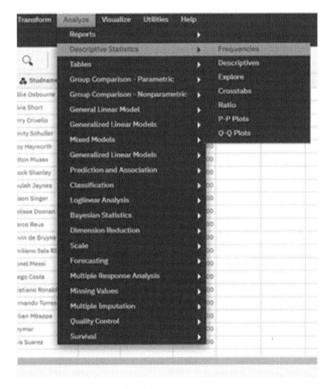

Select Frequencies

Once you have selected Frequencies as shown above, select the variable name that needs to be counted. In this case, we will select the available variable known as schoolname to find out which schools these students go to. Hit the right arrow selected in red to move the Available Variable to the Selected Variable column.

Select the right arrow to move an Available Variable

Once you have confirmed that the variable is in the Selected Variable section, select Run Analysis, as shown below:

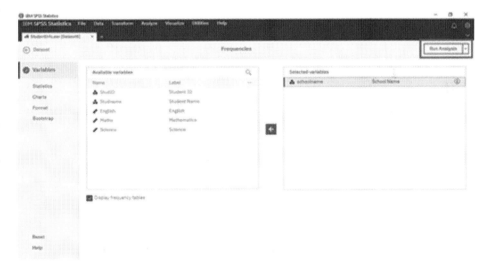

Select Run Analysis to Generate Output

The following output should be available to determine the frequency of the number of students who go to Harvard, Stanford, and Yale.

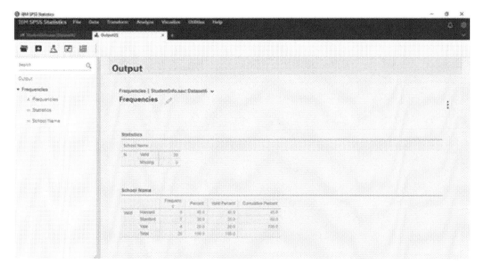

Look at the Statistics & School Name sections

The Statistics as shown in the image above checks to see if all 20 cases were valid or not. In other words, the analysis first checks for missing data before going through with the count. In the second section, you find the breakup of the students who go to Harvard, Stanford, and Yale.

Not only do you get a individual frequency count but both the percent and valid percent is also calculated. The cumulative percent should clue you in on the fact that 100 percent of the data has been used in this frequency analysis.

There's another feature that is worth talking about because this is something that you can use when you run an analysis in SPSS. Since the analysis is compiled in an Output file, you can save this separately for later reference. Select the icon highlighted in red below in order to save this Output file.

Save Output

Once you select the icon as shown above, you'll be taken to a familiar dialog box where you can enter a name for the Output file and then save it for future use. It must be pointed out that Output files have a file extension of .spv, as shown below.

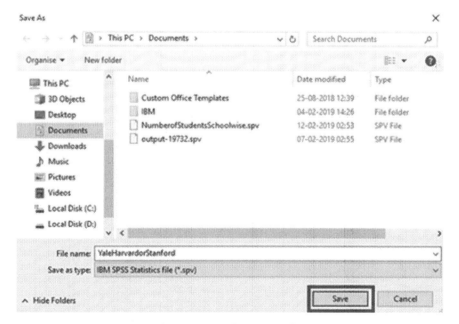

Saving an Output File

Now that we've covered how to use the Frequencies function in the Analyze menu, let's move on to learning how to calculate the measures of central tendency in descriptive statistics.

Measures of Central Tendency

As we learned in the previous chapter, mean, median, and mode are the three measures of central tendency. Let's look at how we can calculate each of these statistics by following the prescribed steps in SPSS for each of these measures. It's really simple.

Mean

As we learned earlier, the mean, in relation to this dataset of university students, can prove to be useful by helping us determine the average for all subjects scored by each student.

So, let us look at the flow of steps necessary to generate the mean of a certain subject taken at the schools of Stanford, Yale, and Harvard. Just remember when you use this function for any other dataset, you can save the Output file if necessary.

Select the Analyze menu and then select Descriptives.

Open the Descriptives Menu

For this purpose, we will calculate the mean of the student scores of a test taken in Python programming and move it from the Available Variables section to the Selected Variables section.

Move the quantitative variable from Available to Selected Variables

After this, select the Options menu under Variables header, as highlighted in red below.

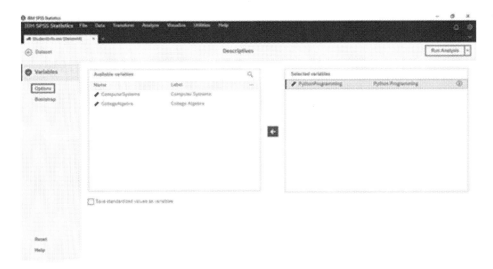

Select Options in order to calculate the Mean

Select Mean under Central Tendency in the Options Menu

Now, select the Run Analysis option in the top right hand corner of your screen and wait for the results:

Select Mean and the Run Analysis option

Once the analysis is complete, you'll find a simple summary of the average for Python programming as well as the count of the number of valid data points in the output.

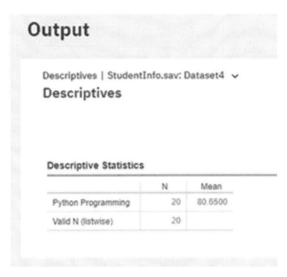

Valid data check and mean of Python Programming calculation

While this might seem rather simple, SPSS is so powerful as a statistical analysis tool that it allows you to calculate the Geometric and the Harmonic mean, as well. This is worth looking into even if you haven't looked at these types of means.

That said, you can perform these calculations once you begin to generate reports using the Case Summaries function.

Median

The median, as we learned, is the value that occupies the center-most position across the distribution of values in the sample that we are evaluating. If two values share this position, we take the mean of these two values and consider that to be the median.

Yet again, calculating the median using SPSS is very simple. But before we begin, we must remember that calculating the median involves counting and arranging the values in ascending order.

In saying that, we will have to go back to Frequencies in the Analyze menu, as shown below.

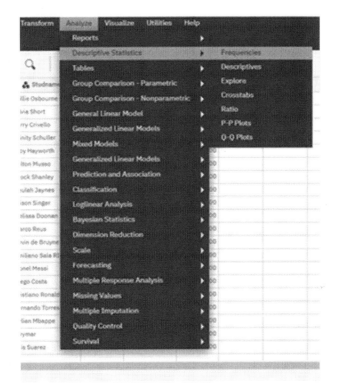

Select the Frequencies option under Descriptive Statistics

Now, move the variable with quantitative data and make sure you uncheck the Display frequency tables option as highlighted in red. The reason why you must do the latter is because you will find the number of occurrences of each value in the Selected Variable. We don't need it when calculating the median of the Selected Variable.

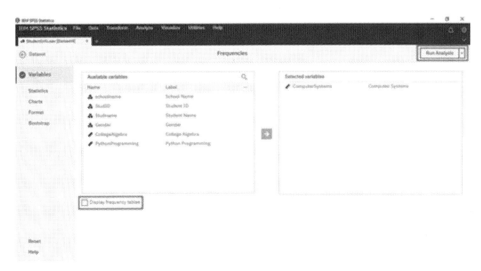

Uncheck the Display Frequency tables at the bottom-left hand corner

Now, select the Statistics option just below the Variables option and select the checkbox labeled Median. After doing this, select Run Analysis to compute the Median of the Selected Variable.

Select Median under Central Tendency

You can find the final calculation of the Median for Computer Systems, as shown in the Output below:

Output

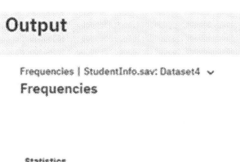

The Median is 80.500

That said, even though we are looking at each of the measures one by one, you don't have to calculate each of these statistics this way. As you get used to SPSS, you will be generating a number of statistics in one go.

Having said that, let's look at how we calculate the final measure of Central Tendency called the Mode next.

Mode

By definition, the mode of any Selected variable involves determining which value has occurred the most number of times. So, in order to calculate the mode, we begin by selecting the Frequencies menu. which is under Descriptive Statistics in the Analyze Menu.

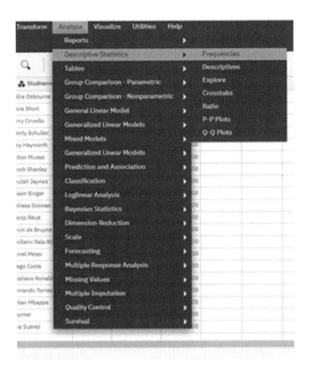

Select the Frequencies option in order to calculate the Mode

Now, select the variable that you wish to calculate the Mode for and move it from the Available Variables section to the Selected Variables section. In this case, we are using the test scores for College Algebra. Also, do not forget to select the Display frequency tables checkbox, as shown below.

Select the Display frequency tables option

Now, select the Statistics option highlighted in red below and select the checkbox that reads as Mode under Central Tendency.

Select Mode and Run Analysis

Now, select Run Analysis after selecting the Mode checkbox and wait for the results.

As shown below in the Output section, the Mode is the quantity 85.00 from the Selected Variable, College Algebra.

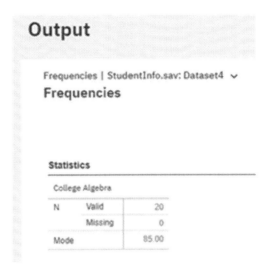

The Mode is 85.00

Since we did select the Display Frequency Tables checkbox, we will also obtain the output that lists all the values in a Frequency Table.

As you can see, the value of 85 occurs thrice, which is why it has been selected as the Mode of this particular variable. Look at the Frequency Table below and you will find out why the quantity of 85 is considered to be the Mode.

College Algebra

		Frequency	Percent	Valid Percent	Cumulative Percent
Valid	72.00	1	5.0	5.0	5.0
	74.00	1	5.0	5.0	10.0
	75.00	1	5.0	5.0	15.0
	79.00	2	10.0	10.0	25.0
	81.00	1	5.0	5.0	30.0
	83.00	2	10.0	10.0	40.0
	85.00	**3**	**15.0**	**15.0**	**55.0**
	88.00	2	10.0	10.0	65.0
	91.00	1	5.0	5.0	70.0
	92.00	1	5.0	5.0	75.0
	95.00	1	5.0	5.0	80.0
	96.00	1	5.0	5.0	85.0
	97.00	1	5.0	5.0	90.0
	99.00	2	10.0	10.0	100.0
	Total	20	100.0	100.0	

The quantity 85.00 occurs thrice in the Output

Now that we have completed the three measures of Central Tendency, let's move on to calculating the Measures of Spread or Dispersion in SPSS.

But before that, if you've made any mistake when calculating the Mean, Median, or Mode, or wish to run the analysis for another Variable, you can select the Reset option as highlighted in red below. Also, if you're not sure what to do next, select Help in order to read more about using this feature in the SPSS Statistics Help page online.

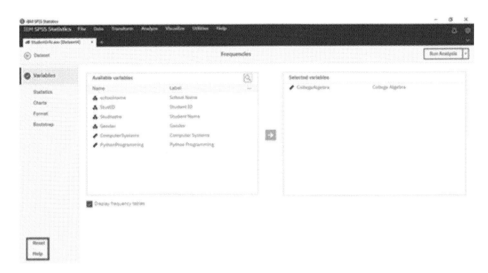

Select the Reset option highlighted in red to start over

One last thing: you can select the Format section under Variables so as to rearrange the display to ascending or descending order.

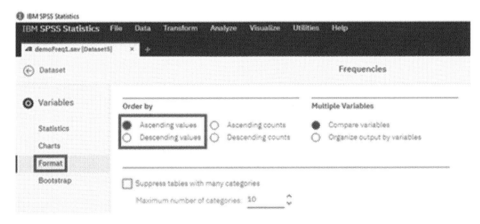

You can list the Output in both ascending and descending order

Now that we've covered the procedures on how to calculate the mean, median, and mode, let us move on to calculating the measures of spread or dispersion.

Measures of Spread

As we learned in the previous chapter, there are three measures of spread or dispersion such as interquartile range, variance, and standard deviation. Let us begin by calculating the Interquartile range for a Selected Variable.

Interquartile Range

For this, we have to go back to the Frequencies sub-menu where you can calculate a number of statistics related to spread or dispersion. So, let's begin with calculating the range and interquartile range of a Selected Variable.

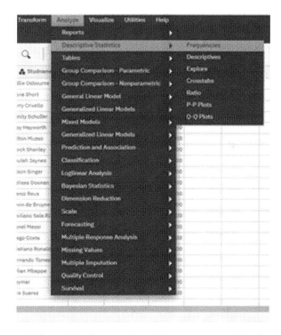

Select Analyze, then Frequencies Path

Once we follow the above path, select the variable that you would like to analyze and move it into the Selected Variables section. Uncheck the Display Frequencies table checkbox in the Variable section.

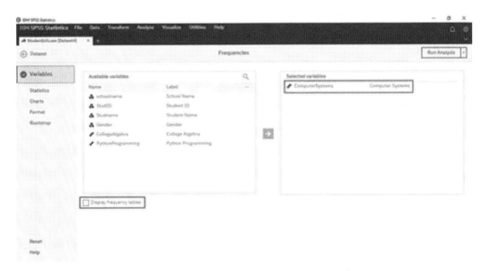

Uncheck the Frequency Tables checkbox

Along with this, select the option Statistics, and select the checkbox titled Quartiles under Percentile Values, as well as the checkboxes titled Range, Minimum, and Maximum under Dispersion.

Select Range, Minimum and Maximum & Quartiles

Once you are done, select Run Analysis highlighted in red at the top right-hand corner of your screen and wait for results. As soon as the analysis is complete, the Output section should display the following statistics:

Frequencies | StudentInfo.sav: Dataset4

Frequencies

Statistics

Computer Systems

N	Valid	20
	Missing	0
Range		37.00
Minimum		62.00
Maximum		99.00
Percentiles	25	71.2500
	50	80.5000
	75	87.5000

Computed Values of Range, Minimum, Maximum and the Interquartile Range

So, why is it important to calculate the interquartile range? In particular, one can use these values to calculate the outliers of any set of values in a variable. But along with this, the z-score of a particular test score can reveal a lot about where that particular test score is placed in an entire variable of values. This is because the z-score of a particular test score here is nothing but the number of standard deviations from the calculated mean.

Having said that, let's now look at how we can calculate standard deviation and variation in the next section and acquaint ourselves with a deeper understanding of what it means to calculate a z-score. It must be pointed out that since the standard deviation of a set of values is derived from the variance calculated, it's good to learn how to obtain these two values simultaneously.

Variance and Standard Deviation

For variance and standard deviation, we can easily calculate both these measures by selecting Descriptive Statistics from Analyze Menu and then the Frequencies sub-menu.

Once you follow this path, move one of the Available Variables to the Selected Variables section. Now, select the Std. Deviation and Variance checkboxes in the Statistics menu as highlighted in red below. After this, select Run Analysis to compute these two values.

Select Std. deviation and Variance in the Statistics Menu

After the output is generated, you can see the values of both the Variance and the Standard Deviation as shown in the image below:

Output

Frequencies | StudentInfo.sav: Dataset4

Frequencies

Statistics

Computer Systems

N	Valid	20
	Missing	0
Std. Deviation		10.20526
Variance		104.147

Values of Variance & Std. deviation

As one can tell, the Standard Deviation measured for this variable of data is very high. As a rule, the higher the standard deviation value, your values of data have a wider spread from the mean. This might not be a good or bad thing as it really depends on the situation from which you have collected data and the action you intend to take based on its results. Outliers in certain sets of data tend to reflect real life accurately.

Now that we know how to calculate both the mean and standard deviation of a set of values, it's time to look at the concept of the z-score.

As mentioned earlier, when we take a single test score in the Selected Variable Computer Systems and want to know how that student has fared in relation to the rest of the class, we calculate the z-score by using the formula: Individual Test Score - Mean divided by Standard Deviation.

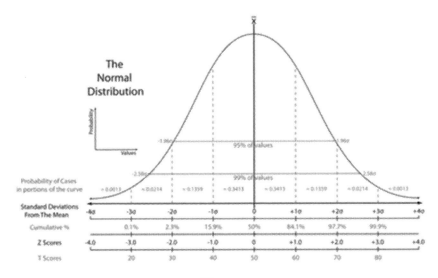

The z-score

So, let's say that Larry's score after taking the Computer Systems test was 86. That's our individual test score. Upon running an analysis to calculate the mean and standard deviation using SPSS, we obtain the values 80.6 and 10.20526.

Upon using the formula, we find out that Larry's z-score is 0.529121. We can round this figure off to 0.53. Now, if we know that the set of values follows the pattern of a normal distribution, we use a Z-table that gives us a value that reflects where Larry stands in comparison to the rest of his classmates.

Since Larry's z-score is positive, we use what is known as the right z-table, which correlated to test scores above the mean. You can find the z-table as this link. We obtain a value of 0.2019. In terms of percentages, actually 20.19 percent of the class did better than Larry.

So, there also exists the probability that a score could be greater than Larry's score for that same percentage. In addition, this also points to the fact that Larry's score was higher than 79.81 percent of the class. That's pretty good, isn't it?

Simply put, if your z-score has a positive and high value when compared against the mean, you're probably one of those who has put a lot of effort into their studies. If you have a negative value (and use the left Z-table correctly), this simply means that your test scores are simply not up to the mark. In other words, being able to calculate dispersion can help us look at how certain scores fare in comparison to others.

But how do you tell whether a distribution is normal or not? A simple test is generally used to determine this by calculating the z-score of the interquartile range values of Q1 and Q3.

When you calculate the z-scores of the interquartile range (Q1 and Q3), you can tell whether the test score values in the analyzed variable form a normal distribution depending on how close the Q1 and Q3 values are to -0.67 and +0.67.

As difficult as this might seem to grasp, we can use the z-score calculations to make predictions as to what score one must get in order to be considered part of the top 10 percent of the class. Of course, this depends on the set of values you are using to analyze and whether or not it forms a Normal distribution or not.

Having said that, there's one more nifty SPSS feature that we can use to actually check whether the values we are analyzing form a normal distribution or not. For this, select the Charts option, highlighted in red below. After this, select the radio button Histograms along with the checkbox titled Show Normal Curve on Histogram.

You can graph Descriptive Statistics when running an analysis

When you select the Run Analysis option and generate the output, you'll find the histogram as shown below with the normal curve shown as well.

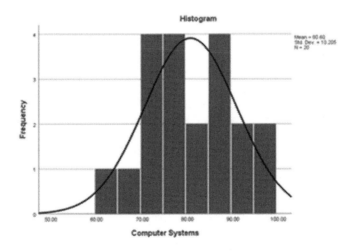

The Histogram is the best chart to display a Normal Distribution

As you can probably tell, this is a distribution with a spread of values that favours the left and is also called a negatively skewed normal distribution. This is clearly indicated by the left tail that is much longer than the right tail.

But we still can't tell by how much?

For that we need to calculate the skewness value, which we will look at in the next section.

Measures of Shape or Distribution

We have discussed the measures of shape, but briefly in the previous chapter. In this one, we will look at how we can calculate values related to both skewness and kurtosis one at a time.

While this chapter seeks to walk you through how one can calculate these basic statistics, it's good to also understand how we can apply statistical thinking to the values we generate.

So, let's look at skewness first and then move on to kurtosis next.

Skewness

In order to calculate the skewness of any analyzed variable, we select Analyze and Descriptive Statistics menus as well as the Frequencies sub-menu. As always, we have to select the variable we want to analyze and move it to the Selected Variable section, as shown below.

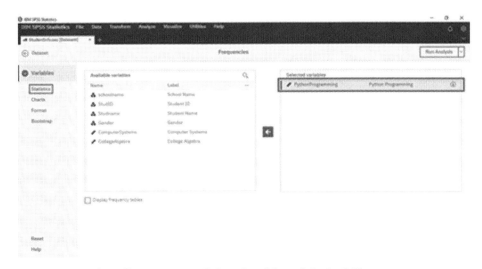

Select Statistics and the checkbox labeled Skewness

In this case, we are using a set of scores that students took when learning how to program in Python. Once you have moved the selected variable, select Statistics as highlighted in red above. Select Skewness and then Run Analysis to generate output in regard to this measure of shape for the selected variable.

Select skewness under Distribution

The output for the variable Python Programming provides us with a measure of skewness that we can use to determine whether this distribution is negatively or positively skewed.

Statistics		
Python Programming		
N	Valid	20
	Missing	0
Skewness		-1.505
Std. Error of Skewness		.512

Value of Skewness and its Std. Error

Based on the value, which is -1.505, we can tell that this distribution is negatively skewed or has a longer left tail. When we calculate the skewness value for the variable Computer Systems, we get the output shown below:

Statistics		
Computer Systems		
N	Valid	20
	Missing	0
Skewness		.057
Std. Error of Skewness		.512

Value of Skewness and its Std. Error for another Variable

So, what should this tell you about the skewness of values in the Computer Systems variable? That it is less skewed compared to the Python Programming set of values.

But there's one more aspect we've not taken into consideration just yet. There's a statistic called Standard Error of Skewness that has also been calculated here, and for good reason too. In statistics, when we analyze a small sample, this gives rise to errors. In order to ensure that we obtain accurate values, we have to calculate a test statistic that is but a ratio of both the skewness and the Standard Error of Skewness values here.

In other words, when we divide 0.057/0.512 we get a skewness of 0.1113 for the Computer Systems variable. So, what does this value of skewness indicate?

As arule of thumb, if you obtain a skewness value that is less than -1 and greater than +1, this is a highly-skewed distribution. If you get a skewness value that is between -0.5 and -1 and +0.5 and +1, then the distribution is moderately skewed. If the skewness value lies between -0.5 and +0.5, the distribution is said to be somewhat symmetric.

One can tell that the Computer Systems distribution of values is approximately symmetric here. In comparison, the Python Programming distribution gives us a skewness value of -2.94, which means that it is highly skewed.

Being able to calculate and interpret skewness can tell us a lot about the data we have at our disposal. It makes our work in statistics to derive meaning and make predictions much harder, since it does not follow the simplest distribution of them all: the Normal distribution.

No matter what, skewness can tell you a lot about your data and should not be underestimated. With that said, we will move on to calculating another measure of shape called kurtosis.

Kurtosis

Kurtosis, we read in a prior chapter, has a lot to do with the distribution's tails. The more outliers you have in a set of values, the longer the tail of your distribution is likely to be. Now, as we did when running an analysis that calculated skewness, we begin by selecting the Analyze and Descriptive Statistics menus, as well as the Frequencies sub-menu.

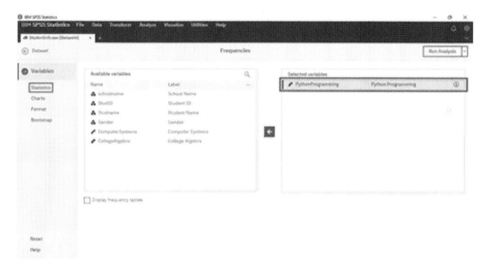

Select Statistics to find Kurtosis

Select Statistics as highlighted in red above and then select the checkbox titled Kurtosis. After this, select Run Analysis and wait for the output to be generated.

Select Kurtosis under Distribution

The output that is generated provides us with the kurtosis value of the variable we have selected for analysis, as shown below:

Statistics

Computer Systems		
N	Valid	20
	Missing	0
Kurtosis		-.448
Std. Error of Kurtosis		.992

Value of Kurtosis and its Std. Error

So, what does the value of -0.448 mean in regard to kurtosis? Is this a measure of high or low kurtosis? Also, what does the standard error of kurtosis value offer here?

As a test for whether the data follows a shape of a normal distribution, we divide the value of kurtosis with its standard error, much like the calculation followed for skewness.

Using the variable Computer Systems, we generate a value of -0.451. So, what does this mean? If we generate a value of less than -2 and greater than +2, the distribution isn't normal. So, one can tell that we're well within those limits for this set of data values.

Now, when we repeat this action for the variable of Python programming test scores, we get the following output:

Statistics

Python Programming		
N	Valid	20
	Missing	0
Kurtosis		1.979
Std. Error of Kurtosis		.992

Kurtosis and Std. Error for another variables

Upon dividing 1.979 by 0.992, we obtain the value of 1.994. Which means that the distribution of values is barely normal in nature.

Yet again, as mentioned in the section on Skewness, if a set of values does not follow the Normal distribution, this makes the statistician's work harder. In this case, since it points to the number of outliers present in the set of values, we might have to go back to the drawing board in order to check whether these outliers were real or are due to human error.

Having said that, there's just one more thing that we need to discuss in order to generate all the descriptive statistics that we have discussed in this chapter.

Using the Case Summaries Section under Reports

While we were able to calculate the measures of central tendency, spread or dispersion and shape on their own, the need to look at all the descriptive statistics in one Output section can prove to be very useful. Better still, if we could further sub-divide the data set for analysis, that would be pretty nifty too, right?

For example, if we wanted to generate all the descriptive statistics that we've learned so far but want to examine the statistics according to gender, we could create a case summary. For this, select the Analyze and Reports menus as well as the Case Summaries sub-menu, as shown below:

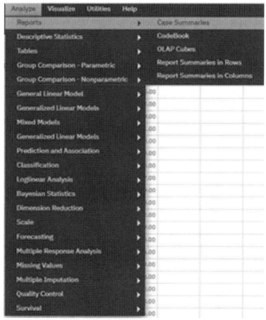

Analyze, Reports and then Case Summaries menus

Once you select Case Summaries, move a numeric variable to the Selected Variables for analysis and a variable that os categorical in nature so as to group and analyze the overall data further. In the example displayed, the three test scores of Computer Systems, College Algebra, and Python Programming will be grouped based on Gender.

In other words, it would be interesting to note whether men or women fared better in each of these subjects and by how much, along with being able to see all the measures in one report.

Run a summary report of all descriptive statistics

If you want to, you can add a title and a caption for this summary report that you are trying to generate in the Options section. When you do, select Run Analysis and wait for the output to be displayed, as shown below:

Case Summaries

Gender		Computer Systems	College Algebra	Python Programming
Female	Mean	78.2000	87.0000	78.9000
	Median	80.5000	86.5000	79.5000
	Range	37.00	27.00	37.00
	Std. Deviation	11.22299	9.88826	10.77497
	Variance	125.956	97.778	116.100
	Kurtosis	-.209	-1.248	1.909
	Skewness	.243	-.218	-1.315
Male	Mean	83.0000	85.6000	82.4000
	Median	82.5000	84.0000	83.0000
	Range	28.00	21.00	31.00
	Std. Deviation	9.00617	6.85079	9.14330
	Variance	81.111	46.933	83.600
	Kurtosis	-.737	-.827	5.326
	Skewness	.279	.223	-2.092
Total	Mean	80.6000	86.3000	80.6500
	Median	80.5000	85.0000	82.5000
	Range	37.00	27.00	37.00
	Std. Deviation	10.20526	8.31042	9.89032
	Variance	104.147	69.063	97.818
	Kurtosis	-.448	-.980	1.979
	Skewness	.057	-.004	-1.505

Case Summaries computes all descriptive statistics in one Output screen

Another option that was considered as a grouping variable to generate a case summary was to be able to examine the data based on the school that they study in. Assuming of course that the tests given to all students were identical.

Having said that, this section seeks to summarize all the measures of descriptive statistics that we've studied so far, which you can see in the image above.

In the next chapter...

We intend to look at the procedures involved in drawing up all the charts available in SPSS based using simple data sets for this purpose. As a beginner, it is just as vital to be able to compute various measures in Descriptive Statistics, yet just as important to select the right type of charts to help us visualize the data itself for inferential purposes. Let's look at as many of them as possible in the next chapter.

*visualize > chart builder > *type of chart**

Chapter Nine

Creating Charts in SPSS

As we have learned so far, one can gain much understanding about a set of values in variables but charts can take that understanding to the next level. Visualizing data is very powerful, as this can help us see trends and correlations vividly. We understand where we have been and where we are and, as a result, we begin to consider what action to take as a result.

SPSS is very useful in this sense as it gives us a wide range of charts to use. From simple histograms to complex Q-Q plots. So that we can visualize our data to summarize it or even use it for the purpose of predictive analysis.

As we dive into this section, please note that we will use the Visualize and Chart Builder sub-menu to draw up all these charts. You can prepare these charts in the Frequencies and Descriptives menus as well. Since we have looked at these types of charts before in the chapter on descriptive statistics, we will also focus on selecting the right type of chart to visualize a set of values correctly.

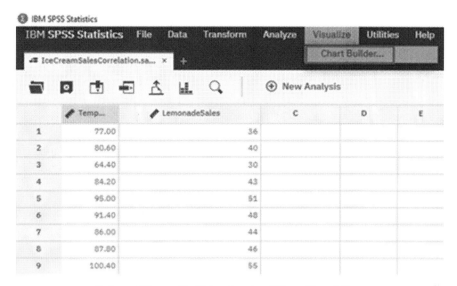

Select Chart Builder in the Visualize Menu

There's another way of accessing the Chart Builder Menu, which involves selecting the quick access icon, as shown in the menu below:

Chart Builder Menu

Having said that, let us look at the procedures involved in constructing some of the most common charts available in SPSS.

Common Graphs Available in SPSS

There are a number of graphs that one will use over and over again in order to visualize descriptive statistics in order to reach conclusions. You would have come across these charts at some point in time or other, given that they have been used in school, business, and at educational institutions as well.

Having said that, we will look at charts such as the Line and Multi-Series graphs, Pie Chart, the Bar Graph, Histogram, Box Plot, and a Scatter Plot.

Line Chart

Let's say you run a clothing store and need to determine at which time of the day you need your staff members to be in at work. There's no point having everyone in if there are no customers, correct?

These are two SPSS variables that we will use in order to chart the data:

Time	Customers
10:00	2.00
11:00	5.00
12:00	10.00
13:00	22.00
14:00	15.00
15:00	5.00
16:00	4.00
17:00	4.00
18:00	3.00

Does a relationship exist between Time & Customers?

For this, let's select the line chart option in Chart Builder to analyze at which time of the day most customers are likely to visit the store in order to purchase an item of their liking. Select Visualize and Chart Builder and then select the Line Chart, as highlighted in red below:

Select the Line Graph Option

Once you select the Line Chart option, select the variables for both the X and Y axis while adding a Primary title and subtitle, as shown below.

You can select the Area option so as to display the area that the data points on the graph covers. Apart from this, you can smoothen out the line by selecting the Smooth option.

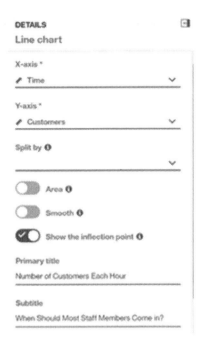

Add the Line Chart Details

Once you have added all Line Chart details, you can see the following line chart displayed:

Highest point in the graph points to 1 PM with 22 customer visits

While this chart might give you a decent picture of when most customers come in, you might need to analyze at least a month's worth of customer visits data in order to find out which hours of the day are the busiest.

If that chart summary is similar to this one, you'll know that it is during the afternoon hours that most, if not all of your staff members, should be present.

Multi-Series Chart

In order to use the multi-series chart, let us select the Visualize menu and Chart Builder.

Month	Year 2010	Year 2011
Jan	163456	163258
Feb	163709	163307
Mar	163982	163351
Apr	164521	163441
May	164255	163722
Jun	163689	163456
Jul	163756	163361
Aug	164091	163688
Sep	163945	164082
Oct	163780	164023
Nov	164088	163937
Dec	163433	163887

Dataset of Unemployed Population

After this, select the Multi-Series option, highlighted in red below:

Select Month as the X-axis

After this, fill in the details in the Multi-Series Chart, as shown below:

Fill in the Chart Title and Subtitle

Make sure you select the option in gray "Add another column" and so add both the years to the Y-axis. Scroll down to the area where you can see the Primary title and the Subtitle, as shown below:

> Primary title
> Unemployment Numbers in the United States
>
> Subtitle
> For the Years 2010 & 2011
>
> Footnote
> please input footnote

Highest & Lowest Unemployment: April 2010 & January 2011

Once you have entered the details, you will find the following multi-series chart where you can find the month during which unemployment was at its highest and lowest for the two years.

You can tell from the chart that for the two years, the lowest unemployment numbers were recorded in January 2011. while the highest unemployment numbers were recorded in April 2010. There is one trend that you can find and which involves the lowest unemployments for each year.

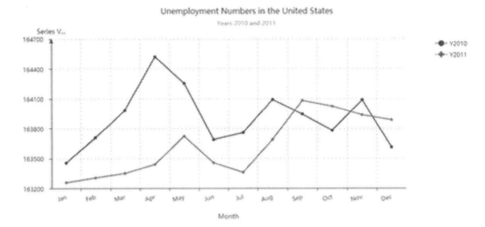

Highest & Lowest Unemployment: April 2010 & January 2011

In January, unemployment was at its lowest for the year, while the months of June and July were much better for jobseekers. For some reason, unemployment numbers rose for both years in the months of April and May and one can attribute it to events that took place at that time.

The recession might be just one incident that comes to mind, which had long-reaching effects for years to come. It might even be because more people might have been working part-time as a result and so were not working during that time of the year. That said, it might be possible that this same trend continues in the following years as well and one must be able to understand what causes the rise and fall of these values.

No matter what, using a multi-series chart here can help you see a trend for both sets of data. You can set up several lines and compare them against each other.

Pie Chart

Each slice of an entire round of cake or pizza represents a percentage. While it is fair to all that you make equal slices when sharing, this isn't always the case in reality.

Especially if you are using a pie chart to visualize the percentage of the total.

Let's say you run a store and want to see the percentage of sales for each of the fruits that you sell every day. Of course, if you obtain regular data on this over time, you should be able to intelligently guess which fruit is most popular amongst customers. Let's just look at sales of one day at your store:

Fruit	Units Sold
Apple	55
Orange	89
Pear	70
Banana	151
Cherry	25
Guava	34
Lemon	102
Plum	48
Grape	60

Fruits sold data for Pie Chart

Now, one must note that we have already counted how many units of fruit have been sold. If you have data for each unit of fruit that you have sold then you will need to count it first.

This isn't a problem because the Pie Chart feature in SPSS gives you the option to calculate the percentages for counted data but also uncounted data as well.

Select the Pie Option as highlighted in red

After this, enter the details in the Pie Chart selecting the Fruit variable for Category and the selecting Sum as shown below. Select Units Sold as the Value.

Select Fruit as the Category

Now, don't forget to enter the Primary title and Subtitle chart details too:

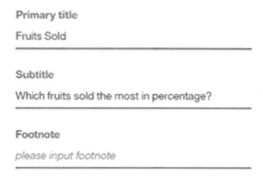

Enter the Primary title and Subtitle here

You can find the Pie Chart as shown below along with the legend located at the right hand side:

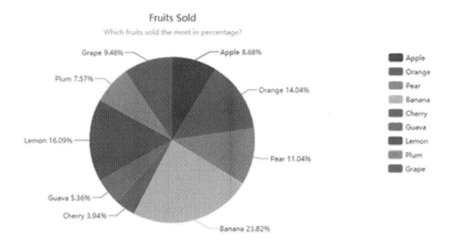

Pie Charts for Fruits Sold

One must point out that the Fruit Sold variable is one that lists discrete categories, much like the Hours and Months we used in the Line and

Multi-Series charts. Still, using a pie chart gives you a clear picture in terms of percentage as to which of these categories perform best.

So, you can tell from this pie chart that the most number of units sold were that of lemons and bananas. One broad conclusion that you can arrive at, as a grocer, is that you need to focus on keeping more units of bananas and lemons compared to guavas and cherries.

Not very differently, if you are trying to analyze sets of data with discrete categories, another option that helps us clearly see the counts is the Bar Graph, which is what we will cover next.

Bar Graph

If one wanted to know how many students amongst a list of 20 attend Harvard, Yale, and Stanford, the bar graph considers each of these universities discrete categories and carries out a count.

	School N...	Student ID	Student Name	Gender	Computer Systems	College Algebra	Python Progra...
1	Yale	0001	Willie Osbourne	Male	79.00	88.00	89.00
2	Harvard	0002	Silvia Short	Female	65.00	92.00	55.00
3	Stanford	0003	Larry Crivello	Male	86.00	95.00	82.00
4	Yale	0004	Trinity Schuller	Female	71.00	97.00	79.00
5	Yale	0005	Troy Hayworth	Male	77.00	83.00	81.00
6	Harvard	0006	Felton Musso	Male	90.00	96.00	83.00
7	Harvard	0007	Brock Shanley	Male	72.00	76.00	79.00
8	Stanford	0008	Beulah Jaynes	Female	83.00	85.00	80.00
9	Stanford	0009	Alison Singer	Female	62.00	74.00	67.00
10	Harvard	0010	Melissa Doonan	Female	70.00	79.00	79.00

Dataset of Computer Science Students

Now, select Visualize and then Chart Builder, and select Bar as shown below:

Select the Bar Chart as highlighted in red

Once you've selected Bar, it's time to enter the Bar chart details as shown below. Make sure you select the variable that you wish to count here. In the dataset displayed above, we will select School Name in the Bar Chart Details section to the left of your screen.

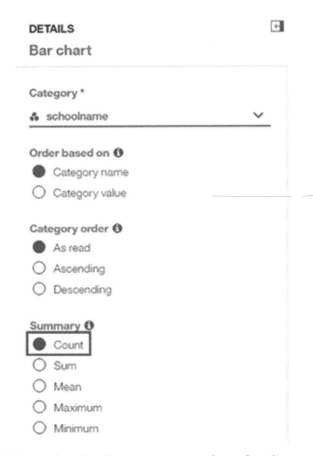

Ensure that the Summary type selected is Count

After you've entered the details, fill in the Chart Title, and the subtitle as shown below:

Primary title

Yale, Harvard or Stanford

Subtitle

Which university has the most students?

Footnote

please input footnote

Enter more information about the study in the footnote

Once this is done, you can see the bar chart which counts the number of students going either to Harvard, Yale, or Stanford, as shown below:

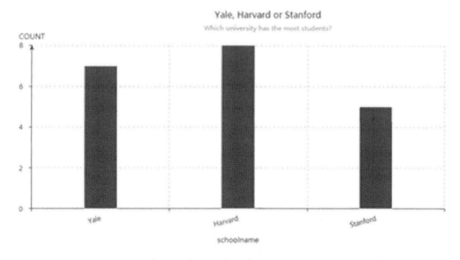

Most students from the dataset go to Harvard

Now, there's another small feature that one can use to include other categories that might shed more light on your analysis using this type of chart. It is called the Split By option that can be found in the Bar Chart Details section.

Use the Split By option to further break down your data

In this dataset, we can also categorize the students as either male or female, so we can use the Gender variable to split the bar chart into both male and female divisions of students who attend these three universities.

You can find the resulting bar chart below:

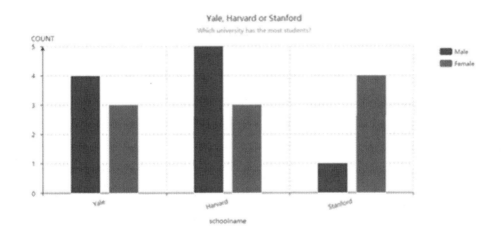

Count of both male and female students going to each university

As you can see, Stanford has the most female students while Harvard and Yale has the same number of female students.

Histogram

While the histogram looks very similar to the bar chart, there is one significant difference. In the case of the former, we will use data that falls into numerical and continuous bins or intervals.

While in the previous example, Yale, Harvard, and Stanford were discrete variables, histograms will show a count of the data that fall into continuous and numerical categories.

For example, if we wanted to categorize the number of students who scored marks between 0 to 100 for a subject like Python programming, we would use a histogram to display the data. In this case, the histogram will create bins of intervals such as 0-10, 10-20 and 20-30, and so on and so forth. As you will see, the intervals are continuous unlike the categories used in creating a bar chart.

Let us use the same dataset that we used to create a bar chart here and are shown below:

	School N...	Student ID	Student Name	Gender	Computer Systems	College Algebra	Python Progra...
1	Yale	0001	Willie Osbourne	Male	79.00	88.00	59.00
2	Harvard	0002	Silvia Short	Female	65.00	92.00	55.00
3	Stanford	0003	Larry Crivello	Male	86.00	95.00	82.00
4	Yale	0004	Trinity Schuller	Female	71.00	97.00	79.00
5	Yale	0005	Troy Heyworth	Male	77.00	83.00	81.00
6	Harvard	0006	Felton Musso	Male	90.00	96.00	83.00
7	Harvard	0007	Brock Shanley	Male	72.00	75.00	79.00
8	Stanford	0008	Beulah Jaynes	Female	83.00	85.00	80.00
9	Stanford	0009	Alison Singer	Female	62.00	74.00	67.00
10	Harvard	0010	Melissa Doonan	Female	70.00	79.00	79.00

Dataset of Computer Science Students

Now, select Visualize and Chart Builder, and then select Histogram as highlighted in red below:

bins = intervals

Student scores
↳ histogram

Select Histogram in the Chart Builder Menu

Once you've selected Histogram as shown above, you'll be directed to a screen where you have to enter the Histogram Details, as shown below. Since we are analyzing the Python Programming scores of students who go to Harvard, Yale, and Stanford, select that variable that contains their scores.

Also, do not forget to enter the details for the Primary title and the Subtitle as shown above.

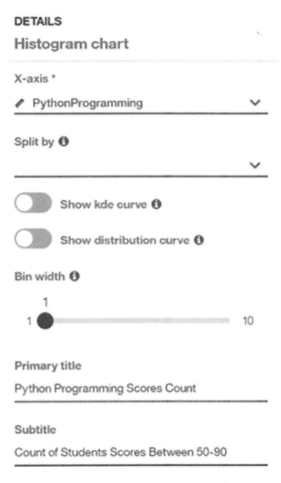

Enter Histogram Chart - Details

After you complete this, you'll find the count of students who scored between 50 to 100 in Python Programming.

Use the Split By option to further split your results for analysis

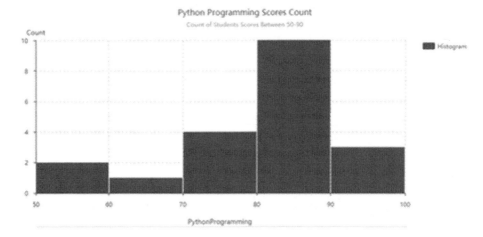

Ten students recorded scores between 80 and 90 in Python Programming

Now, you can use the Split By option here as well in order to further break down the data for this analysis. In this case, we will count how many students from each university scored between 50 to 100.

Use this option to further break down your data for analysis

In this case, we will select School Name in order to obtain a break up of the histogram as shown below:

Add the Variable SchoolName

Upon doing this, we will find that the histogram splits the Python Programming data by each school, as shown below:

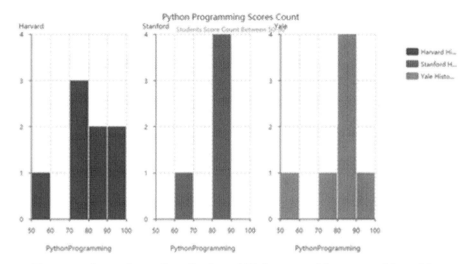

Four students from Stanford and Yale scored between 80 to 90

As you can see, more students did better at Python programming at Stanford and Yale for this very same test.

The Box Plot, as we found, is a graph that is commonly used to display the spread of a distribution's values namely the minimum, first quartile, median, third quartile, and the maximum. Yet another value that will be shown are outliers present in the set of values chosen for the analysis.

Let us use the dataset containing the scores of students to demonstrate how we can use this chart to understand the spread of the data better:

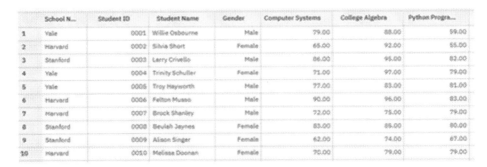

Dataset of Computer Science students

Select Visualize and Chart Builder, and then select the down arrow highlighted in red to reveal all charts available in SPSS:

Select the downward pointing arrow

Once you do this, a list of 21 Charts is shown, from which we will have to pick the Box Plot chart as shown below:

Select Box Plot as highlighted in red

Once you've selected Box Plot, you should enter the details in the Box Plot Chart Details section as shown below. Do NOT use the Split By and Add Another Column options just yet.

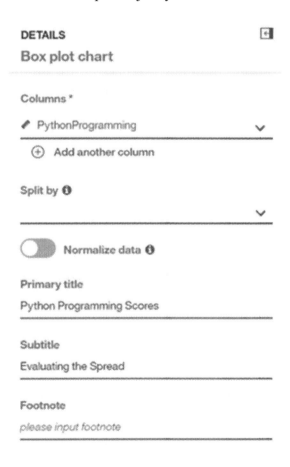

As you can see to the right of your screen, the box plot has been prepared, as shown below:

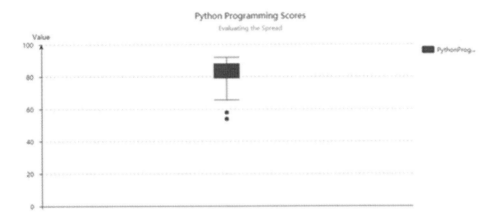

The Box Plot with Two Outliers

When you run your mouse pointer over the whiskers, the two dots and the box itself, you will find the five values that we learned under Measures of Spread or Dispersion calculated here.

If you want to look at the data more closely, you can add another column of data to analyze two scores at a time. For this, we will add Computer Systems as another column in the field shown below:

⊕ Add another column

Select this to add another column of data

Now, add another column for analysis much like Computer Systems here:

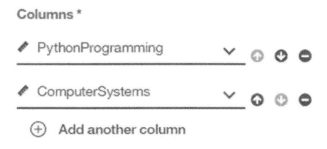

Another Column added for analysis

Now, you should find two box plots side-by-side and which have distinct colors as a way to differentiate between the two. Also, run your mouse over both box plots to find the five measures of spread and outliers if there are any.

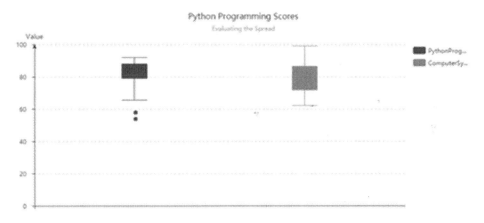

Two separate Box plots that you can analyze for values side-by-side

Finally, you can use the Split By feature when exploring one column of data in order to separate the data even further. In this instance, we will split the data schoolwise and look at the measures of spread that are generated for the Python Programming scores.

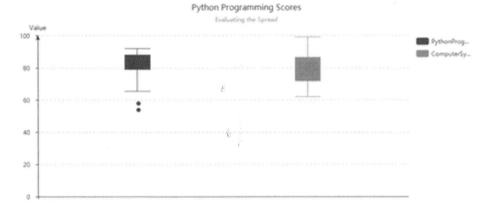

Three separate Box Plots to analyze data by university

Scatter Plot

In this type of graph, you will plot two variables against each other and will draw conclusions based on whether SPSS finds a positive, negative, or no correlation.

But before we look at the procedure, a positive correlation is one where upon the increase of one variable, the second variable increases in value. A negative correlation means that when one variable increases, the other decreases. Finally, if the variables do not form a negative or positive correlation, there is none.

That said, where a correlation exists, we use a line of best fit to indicate this. This line lies as close as possible to all the data points and, in doing so, represents the data in the best possible way.

In order to demonstrate the use of a scatter plot, we will use the following variables so as to look for a correlation. We want to know if an increase or decrease in temperature affects lemonade sales. In this case, the temperature is the independent variable while lemonade sales is the dependent variable.

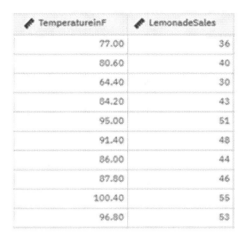

Dataset for Lemonade sales and Temperature

Now, select Visualize and Chart Builder and then select Scatter as shown below:

Select the Scatter Plot graph as highlighted in red

Once you do this, select the independent variable for the X-axis and the dependent variable for the Y-axis. Also, enter the Primary Title and Subtitle as well.

Select among the options for the line of best fit

Always make sure you enter the details for the Primary title, Subtitle, and the Footnote.

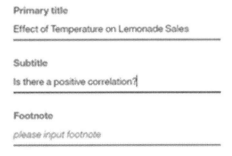

Never forget to enter the chart details

Once you finish entering these details, you will find the scatter plot chart to the right hand side of your screen.

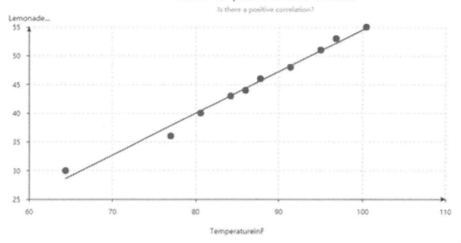

The Line of Best Fit

One can tell that there exists a positive relation between temperature and lemonade sales, as shown above.

Up until now, we have looked at charts that are commonly used in statistics. So, let us continue looking at a few others that SPSS offers and which might be of use when conducting data analysis.

Other Charts Available in SPSS

Even if we have explored all the charts that were discussed when covering descriptive statistics, it would be nice to look at less common types of graphs that can be used to visualize data.

Population Pyramid Chart

This type of chart, while being a combination of histograms placed back-to-back, helps us find the distribution of the population based on a category such as gender and age. In order to demonstrate how this type of chart can be created, let us analyze a dataset of students taking Computer Science from Yale, Harvard, and Stanford.

Dataset of Computer Science Students at Yale, Harvard and Stanford

Using this dataset, we are going to build a population pyramid chart that evaluates the age of both male and female students. Once you select Visualize and Chart Builder, select the Population Pyramid chart option as shown below:

Select the Population Pyramid Chart

Once you do this, select the variables that you want to compare and add them to both the x-axis and y-axis. For this analysis, we are comparing the age and gender of students at Yale, Harvard, and Stanford. Also, ensure you add an appropriate Primary Title and Subtitle.

Population Pyramid Chart - Details

Once you complete this, the population pyramid chart can be seen as shown below:

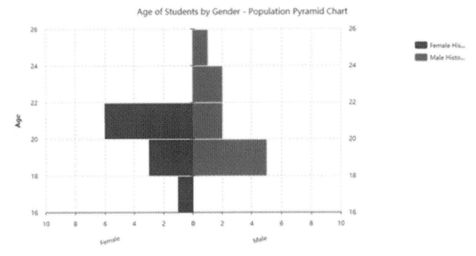

Age vs. Gender Analysis

From the data, we can see that six women attend college between the age of 20-22 while five men attend these colleges between the ages of 18-20. On the whole, there are no women at university after the age of 22 years, while there five men who are pursuing an education after that age.

Treemap Chart

This type of chart can help us visualize data and the hierarchy that exists within the dataset. Using the dataset of Computer Science student scores, we might want to know how many men or women go to each university.

Dataset of Computer Science Students

Using the dataset shown above, select Visualize and Chartbuilder, and then select Treemap as shown below:

Select the down arrow and then the Treemap Chart

Once you do, select the variables whose hierarchy you would like to look at. So, based on the variables in the given dataset, select the School Name and Gender variables, as shown below:

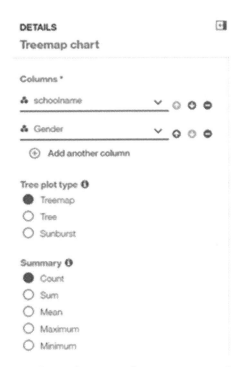

Count the number of men and women at each university

Enter the details in the Primary Title and Subtitle section too, as shown below:

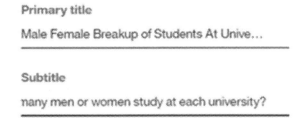

Always enter the details in the charts you use

Once this is done, you will find the Treemap with the following hierarchy that counts the number of males and females at each university in this dataset:

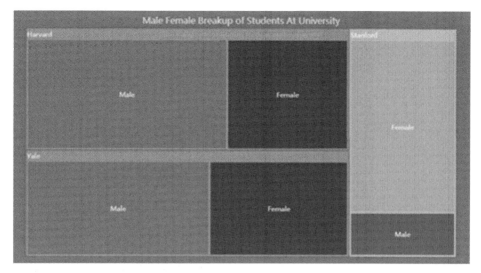

The TreeMap Chart displaying Gender at each University

If you move the mouse pointer over each of these segments, you will find the frequency of the men or women at Harvard, Stanford, and Yale.

Now, let's look at another chart that can compare several sets of numerical variables and reveal correlations or patterns in the dataset.

Parallel Chart

Commonly used in the academic profession to analyze the correlation between variables, it is best used for variables that contain numerical data. We will use the dataset that contains the information of the scores of Computer Science students in Computer Systems, Python Programming, and College Algebra.

parallel chart

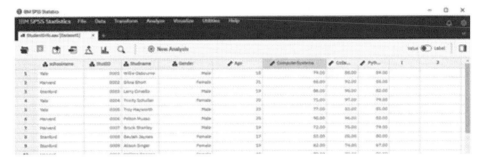

Dataset of Computer Science students

In order to access this chart type, select Visualize and Chart Builder and then select Parallel, as shown in the image below:

Select the Parallel Chart

Once you do this, enter the columns that consists of numerical data in order to draw the lines across their respective axes. In this case, we are going to select College Algebra, Computer Systems, and Python Programming, as shown below. Don't forget to enter a Primary Title and Subtitle. Also, do not select any categorical variable type in the Color Map section.

Parallel Chart - Details

Now, look at the Parallel chart displayed to the right of your screen and as shown below:

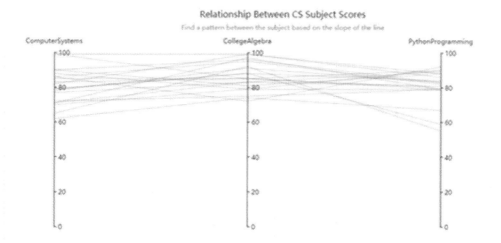

If the slope of several lines match, a correlation exists

As for the Color Map field, you can use it to deepen your analysis by school, gender, or age. In this case, one can evaluate whether age matters when seeing the correlation of these three scores. So, for the purpose of this analysis, let us select the Age variable in the Color Map.

Use Color Map to group and analyze data

When you do this, several colors are used for different lines based on the individual age of each student whose scores are being analyzed.

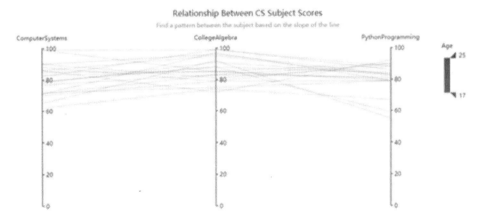

The varying color lines display the age

In other words, we can segregate the lines according to the age intervals and inspect it for patterns within that age group. That said, this is an example of multivariate analysis because we compare two variables but further refine the analysis by selecting a variable that is categorical in nature.

206

In the next chapter...

Now that we've covered the types of charts that you can use to visualize data to obtain summary values in Descriptive Statistics, let us move on to deepening our knowledge in the area of Inferential Statistics.

Chapter Ten

Introduction to Inferential Statistics

By virtue of the term infer, we come to understand that the branch of inferential statistics has to do with making predictions based on data available. A large part of inferential statistics has to do with understanding probability and the existence of distributions for both discrete and continuous values which we can use to determine expected values or intervals.

The mathematical approach to finding probability began with a gambling dispute

Still, one must take note of the fact that our understanding of inferential statistics and its methods to determine the accuracy of population parameters depends on our understanding of descriptive statistics. As mentioned in an earlier chapter, the goal of inferential statistics is to draw conclusions about the entire population from the samples that we analyze.

Just one case in a data sample of football fans

This is because if you wanted to know for sure if all men in Europe liked football or not, you can't simply conduct a survey that collects all their views on such a matter. It's just not feasible. As a result, samples are selected and analyzed for its parameters. In order to carry out these calculations, certain assumptions have to be made apart from the need to include probability as a factor in the final inference. Still, one must admit that we will never accurately calculate what these parameters will be, not unless we go ahead and collect information from every member of the population.

Sample, Population, & Random Sampling

So, what is a sample and the population?

The dataset containing students scores that we used earlier contained variables that were both numeric and categorical in nature. Simply put, the dataset of 20 university students from three Ivy League universities. This is, as we should know by now, a sample. In comparison, the entire population would be all the students pursuing a Computer Science degree at Yale, Stanford, and Harvard.

So, what can this dataset tell us about the population of Computer Science students? Very little or nothing if we cannot obtain a sample that mirrors the data or the statistics generated from the population in equal proportion. It really depends on selecting random samples from the population that is said to represent it equally.

When you calculate statistics for these samples, it should be expected that it will not exactly produce the same value as the population mean but will be more or less the same. This is because the sample is nothing but a subset of the population itself with its own unique standard deviation and mean. That said, the data collected in every sample is influenced by chance, which is why including probability as a quantitative factor plays a big role in helping us make inferences in studies about the entire population.

The Central Limit Theorem

Now, there's a fundamental theorem in inferential statistics that makes the assumption that upon analyzing more and more random samples, the statistics calculated follow the shape of a Normal distribution.

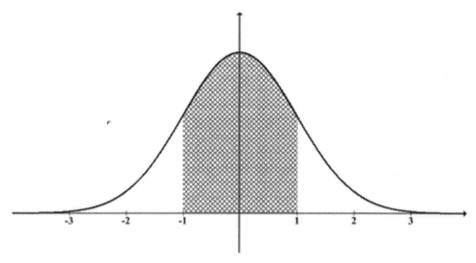

The Normal Distribution

In other words, the mean of every sample considered can be taken as a unique distribution of values whose mean value or expected value will be nothing but the population mean itself. Usually, this theorem takes effect at very high sample sizes from 50 upwards.

In addition, we can calculate the Standard Error of the Mean, which is nothing but the standard deviation of this distribution of values. This value is usually smaller than the actual population standard deviation. In this instance, it isn't like the accurate value of the mean that we discussed earlier.

The master of inference himself - Holmes!

Apart from this, there are other values that are usually estimated in statistical inference such as the population proportion that is usually a percentage, the difference between two population proportions and means. There are specific reasons why one would want to compare different populations which differs from study to study. We can find features in SPSS that helps us run these tests. Of course, the variables would have to be independent and follow the shape of a Normal distribution.

As we have discussed the Normal distribution previously, one must remember that this theorem is particularly influential because, even if the values of the samples themselves do not follow the shape of this distribution, it will not matter.

Inferential Statistics: so what does your data tell you?

Having said that, most datasets that you will use if you take inferential statistics seriously takes on the shape of a Normal distribution and is a condition that will allow people to carry out tests.

Probability Distributions

Now, the Normal distribution is not the only probability distribution that exists. There are several others that are commonly use, which are broadly categorized into two classes: discrete and continuous quantitative values.

An example of Discrete Values

By definition, these probability distributions are very important since they deal with the possibilities of certain occurrences that result in certain outcomes in any experiment. The Binomial, Negative Binomial, and Poisson distributions as well as the Exponential and Uniform distributions are commonly used to calculate the Expected Value and Variance of the distribution of values themselves.

Understanding these types of distributions and being able to use them in real life problems that reflect the distribution's trends is very important in inferential statistics.

Approaches Used in Inferential Statistics

One approach that inferential statistics over time is point estimation and that is generally derived from statistical models. The objective is to derive single values of population parameters. Of course, there are times when these population statistics or parameters cannot be obtained, which is why interval estimation is also considered another approach in inferential statistics.

A minute consists of a time interval of sixty seconds

While the former considers bias and minimum mean squared error as properties that reduce accuracy, the latter adopts confidence intervals, which has made it one of its most popular approaches. That said, statisticians, in general, prefer interval estimation because of the degree of confidence that comes with such calculations in indicating where the population parameter lies. Population proportion is one of the parameters that is commonly estimated using this method too.

When it comes to hypothesis testing, we use the null and alternative hypothesis to make statements about our experiments. Making the right statistical assumptions about the sample values is just as important as selecting the right test statistic that will either reject or validate the null or alternative hypothesis. P-scores are important to decision-making, which is something that one will have to consider at some point in this process of hypothesis testing.

In the next chapter...

Now that we've covered certain important aspects of Inferential Statistics, let us look at a few common procedures that apply both estimation and hypothesis testing as used in inferential analysis in SPSS.

Chapter Eleven

Using SPSS for Inferential Statistics

As we discussed in the previous chapter, there are powerful features that are available in SPSS which can be used to work on generating results that are inferential in nature.

Even if this is a book that covers the basics of statistics and seeks to help beginners also make use of SPSS, it wouldn't be complete without covering features for inferential statistics that SPSS offers its subscribers.

For starters, just like statistics itself is broken down into both descriptive and inferential statistics, the latter is broken into two methods itself: estimation, and hypothesis testing. For estimation, we not only try to obtain the value of a population parameter but also try to estimate the interval of numbers that this parameter's value exists between.

As for hypothesis testing, we attempt to determine the statistical significance or relationship between two sets of variables. When examining the relationships between variables, we not only want to find there exists a positive or negative relationship but how strong it is and also whether it is reliable and relevant.

So, let's begin by understanding how to run an estimation test in SPSS, after which we will look at hypothesis testing.

Estimation

As mentioned in an earlier chapter, there are two types of estimations, which include point and interval estimation. While point estimation attempts to find the exact value of the parameter, interval estimation will not only find a value but the output will also provide you with a confidence interval that is greater and smaller in value than that parameter.

Since the accuracy of point estimation is generally debatable, statisticians prefer interval estimation, since this involves an additional computation: the confidence interval. With this new value, one can tell whether or not the population parameter in question truly lies within these two random intervals.

That said, since the study of inferential statistics depends on accuracy to compute population parameters, interval estimation seems be to more dependable. No one would want to use an incorrect estimation of a parameter to draw wrong conclusions. There is another reason why interval estimation is considered to be risk-averse: by nature, it is said to be closer to hypothesis testing, which we look at later.

So, now let's illustrate how interval estimation in SPSS works by examining the data of 474 employees. It's pretty simple, really!

Now, before we begin to look at the procedure, let us understand what we are looking for in this dataset. As mentioned earlier, we are looking for the average number of years that employees have spent at university in order to find full-time jobs. No, not just employees whose records are present in this dataset but of the entire population of employees in a country like the United States.

So, we begin by selecting the Analyze and the Descriptive Statistics menu and then selecting the Explore option, as shown below.

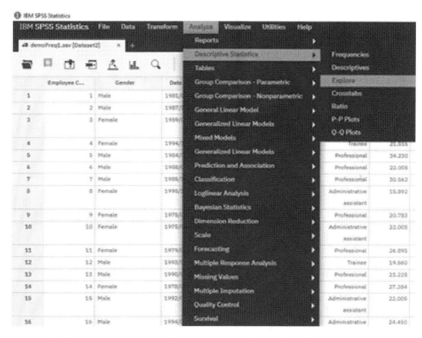

Select Descriptive Statistics and the Explore menus

After this, we will add the number of years in education to the Dependent List. Select Statistics after this. Finally, select Run Analysis as highlighted below.

Add the numeric variable to the Dependent List and select Statistics

Once you have selected Run Analysis, wait for the Output as shown below:

Mean highlighted in red; Confidence Interval highlighted in green

As discussed earlier, we now have the Population Mean as well as the Confidence Interval for this value. Since the Confidence Interval is at 95%, we can be 95% sure that the Population Mean exists between those two values as highlighted in green. Finally, if you want to increase the confidence level to higher values, this works too. It would be wiser to select lower confidence intervals if you want a more accurate value of the true population mean.

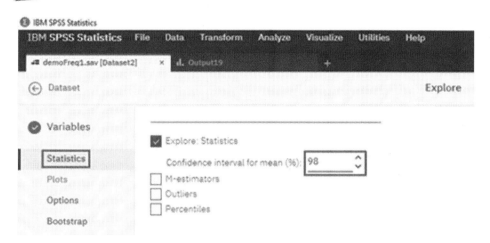

Confidence Interval highlighted in green

That said, there's more that we can do with this, which involves introducing a factor that helps us find the true population mean based on this very factor. In this instance, let us find the average years spent at university by employees based on gender.

For this, we will have to add another variable so as to split the information into two different sections. In other words, we hope to calculate the true population mean of the average years spent at university for men and women.

As shown below, add gender to the Factor List and select Run Analysis.

average scores for exp/control schools

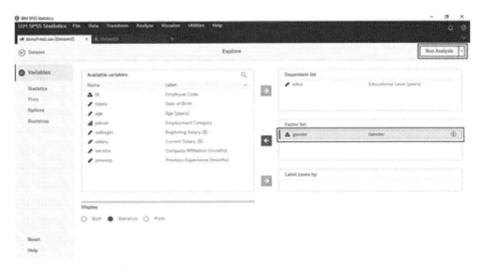

Add a categorical variable to the Factor list

Once you do so, wait for the results as shown in the Output section below:

Split Means highlighted in red; Split Confidence Intervals in green

As you can see, the true population mean has been calculated for both male and female employees along with a confidence interval of 98%. In other words, you can be sure that the true population mean of the number of years spent at university by men and women lies between the respective confidence intervals.

So, this is one simple example as demonstrated in SPSS as to how one can calculate a population parameter based on a sample. Next, we will look at hypothesis testing and understand why this is so important in inferential statistics.

Hypothesis Testing

Now, inferential statistics isn't just for calculating parameters but to also test a hypothesis by using statistical methods that have been developed over time. In particular, we want to know if there exists a relationship between two variables, but most importantly, we want to know if this relationship is real or not.

This is done by setting a null or alternative hypothesis where the former clearly states that there is no relationship between the two. In other words, it is false. The latter confirms that there does exist a relationship or the claim made is true, which is based on reliable computations.

Once you have set up the two hypotheses, you then get to work to calculate the probability value (or p-value) of the experiment so that we can choose between the null or alternative hypothesis.

As for outcomes, you can either reject the null hypothesis instead of the alternative hypothesis or not reject the null hypothesis in favor of the alternative hypothesis, as evidence might not be available to negate the null hypothesis here.

Even if hypothesis testing is well set up so that you can determine whether a relationship exists based on the p-value that you calculate, there is still a chance for human error, since we don't always obtain a p-value that helps us make solid conclusions. Especially in the case where it lies marginally around the 0.05 p-value.

Classified as Type I and II error, the first type of error is when one rejects the null hypothesis despite being true while the second type of error involves not rejecting the null hypothesis when it is false. Experts conclude that the Type I Error is far more serious than that of a Type II error which usually occurs due to the analysis of small sample sizes.

Now, based on our basic understanding of Hypothesis Testing, we are going to make the claim that the true mean of the population of employees based on our previous samples is 27 years old.

Null Hypothesis: This supports the claim in stating that the population mean is equal to the test variable.

Alternative Hypothesis: This hypothesis states that there does exist a difference between the population mean and the test value selected.

Now, before we begin, the objective of running this test is to obtain a p-value. So, let's select the Analyze and Group Comparison - Parametric menus as well as the option labeled One Sample T-Test in order to carry out the analysis.

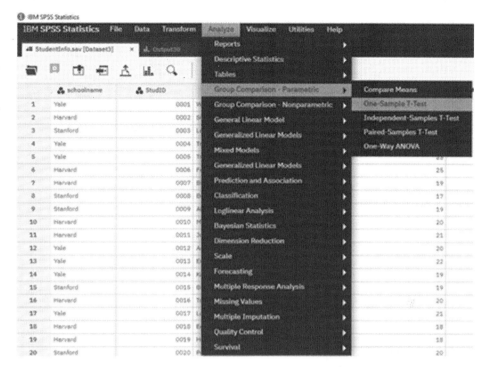

Select Analyze, Group Comparison - Parametric and One Sample T-Test

Once we select this option, the next thing to do is enter the Test Value and select Run Analysis, as shown below:

Enter the Test Variable and the Test Value as highlighted in red

Once you do this, wait for the results where you can locate the p-value. You can find the value obtained under Sig. (2-tailed), as shown below:

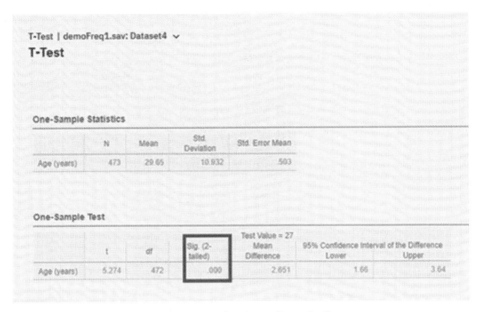

Find the p-value under Sig. (2-tailed) category

Now, how does one interpret this value and validate whether the null or alternative hypothesis is the right choice?

As a rule, if the p-value obtained is less than 0.05, this suggests strong evidence against the null hypothesis. On the other hand, if you obtain a value that is much greater than 0.05, this points to weak evidence against the null hypothesis. Of course, if you get a value that is very close to 0.05, then this is inconclusive.

Since we obtained a value that is less than 0.05, this means that we have to reject the null hypothesis in favor of the alternative hypothesis. In other words, the value 27 is not equal to the population mean.

Now, this isn't the only test that can be performed where you compare a value against a mean. There are tests that allow you to test two means that are either independent or dependent variables. In fact, you can take this even further by testing for three means and more by making the One-Way ANOVA selection as shown in the Group Sample - Parametric above.

Other SPSS Features Available in Inferential Statistics

Since we looked at two examples that dealt with estimation and hypothetical testing, let us look at some other features that are available in SPSS that help us draw important inferences about the datasets that we are using.

Correlation Analysis

Correlation Analysis deals with testing the relationship between two continuous variables in order to see if a relationship exists or not. Better still, it also checks to see which direction the relationship is headed in. In other words, whether it is positive or negative. The strength of the relationship in such a test is expressed as Pearson's r coefficient which ranges between +1 and -1. The closer the values are to +1 or -1, the strength of the relationship tends to be perfect. As the coefficient comes closer to zero, it reduces in strength. Simply put, if you obtain a Pearson's r value of zero, there is no relationship.

As for the output in SPSS, a p-value that is smaller than 0.05, as shown below, means that there exists a strong relationship between the two. The strength of correlation as signified by Pearson's Coefficient below shows that there exists a strong relationship between these two variables.

Correlations			Beginning Salary ($)	Current Salary ($)
Beginning Salary ($)	Pearson Correlation		1	.880**
	Sig. (2-tailed)			.000
	N		474	474
Current Salary ($)	Pearson Correlation		.880**	1
	Sig. (2-tailed)		.000	
	N		474	474
**. Correlation is significant at the 0.01 level (2-tailed).				

Correlation Analysis can be conducted by following the path

Factor Analysis

Factor analysis helps us determine the structure between the correlation of a number of variables in our dataset. This is very useful if we have a large number of variables in our dataset and that can be reduced to dimensions.

In order to carry out this analysis, you have to verify if the following conditions are met: continuous variables, linear associations with each other, a large sample size, and no outliers. Without going into too much detail, the two tests that are usually conducted for Factor analysis include the Kaiser-Meyer-Olkin Measure of Sampling Adequacy and the Bartlett's Test of Sphericity.

Regression Analysis

Finally, we look at regression analysis and the most common types that are available in SPSS. Linear, logistic, multinomial, ordinal, and Poisson regression analysis are the types that we can use based on the types of variables that you wish to use in your analysis, as well as the desired outcome. Once again, this type of analysis also seeks to confirm the existence of a relationship between a dependent variable and a number of other independent variables.

When we use this predictive technique, we examine how each of or a combination of these independent variables affect the dependent variable. Not only can we use this type of analysis for forecasting and time series modelling but also to establish causal relationships. That said, given the numerous regression models available for use, one must take care to select one of these types so as to meet the objectives set prior to using this inferential statistics technique.

In the next chapter...

Now, that we've looked at the two branches of inferential statistics that are used to compute parameters of populations, as well as the approach to determine practical and reliable relationships between two variables, let us briefly look at using Syntax commands in SPSS.

Chapter Twelve

Using SPSS Syntax Commands

As we conclude our journey with IBM SPSS, there's one last topic that we must cover. Even if some people might not be familiar with writing code. it's the Syntax commands that can be used to automate data analysis.

Picture yourself using SPSS at a firm that requires you to conduct data analysis and send your supervisors weekly, monthly, and quarterly reports. Now, this could be simple, much like summarizing the week's sales. Or even making predictions for the upcoming weeks ahead.

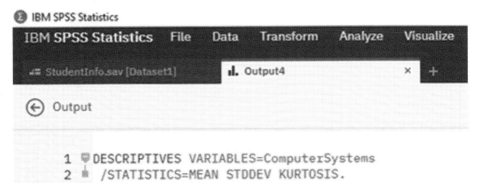

Syntax file - An Example

Without the Syntax commands, you'll have to point-and-click, point-and-click, and point-and-click week in week out. Isn't that just dreary? So, in order to alleviate SPSS users from this source of grief, saving certain point-and-click actions of yours in the form of Syntax commands makes it easy for you to just run a long procedure of commands without having to do anything at all.

Think of this as running a batch file in Windows or even a Linux script that allows you to run a series of commands that you generally perform every other day. Yet, it's that cool!

At this point, you might be thinking: I don't know how to code, so how do I save a Syntax command file so as to run these actions every day, week, or month?

You really don't have to know how to code, since with every point-and-click action you make, SPSS generates code that you can save in an .sps file.

Having said that, let's run through the procedure that helps you do just this. As for those who are familiar with Python programming, you can take automation even further by using scripts that can shorten the code in your Syntax command files.

Python 3 - The languages for data analysis

Creating and Using Syntax Command Files

Now, let say you want to create a Syntax command file that you would like to run to calculate the mean, variance, and kurtosis of a dataset.

How would you do this?

As we learned in earlier sections, as you select menus and submenus to carry out a calculation, Syntax code gets generated in the background.

In order to access this code, all you have to do is wait for the Output to finish running so that you can copy and paste the Syntax commands into a file. Much like the dataset and Output files, we can also create and run Syntax files too.

Let us look at at how we can create a Syntax file and then look at how we can run it from the File menu for different datasets.

Creating a Syntax File

As mentioned earlier, let's say you want compute the mean, variance, and kurtosis of a dataset. Now, this dataset could vary every other week due to the addition of new cases and variables. SPSS allows you to create a Syntax file that you can use to compute the same values on another dataset too. Make sure you save every Syntax file for each dataset you use it for.

Now, let's say we want to calculate these statistics for a variable Computer Systems that consists of scores of Computer Science students at Yale, Harvard, and Stanford. As usual, we would go to the Analyze and Descriptive Statistics menus and select Descriptives, as shown below:

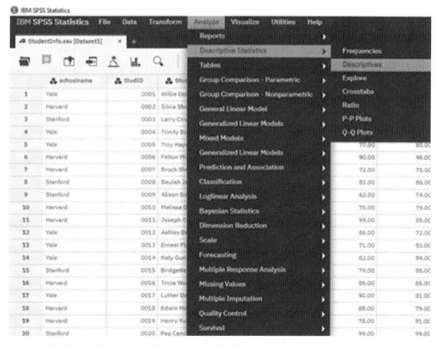

Select Analyze, Descriptive Statistics and Descriptives

Now, move the variable to the Select Variables section and move to the Statistics menu as highlighted in red below:

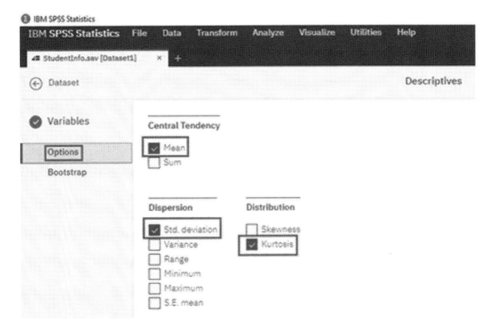

Select the Options Menu and the checkboxes labeled Mean, Std. Deviation, and Kurtosis

Now, once you have done this, select Run analysis and wait for the results. Look for the Edit Syntax option, as highlighted in red in the image below:

Select Edit Syntax as highlighted in red

Once you select Edit Syntax, a new screen opens up with a series of Syntax commands, as shown below:

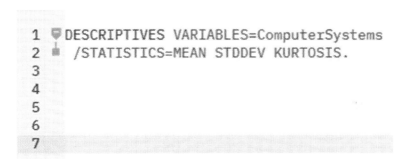

Syntax Code for Calculating Mean, Std. Deviation, and Kurtosis

Select this code with your mouse and then paste it into a new Syntax file that you can open in the File menu:

Copy and Paste this Code into a New Syntax File

In order to paste this code, you will need to open a new Syntax file by using thefollowing path, as shown below:

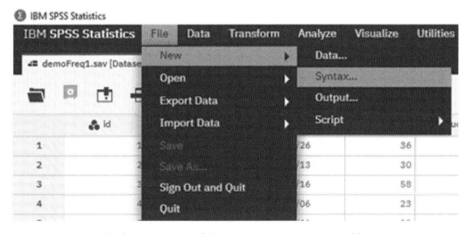

Select New and Syntax to open a new file

This is what a new Syntax file looks like:

A New Syntax file

Now, once you do this, paste the code into this file and save it by selecting Save As in the File menu.

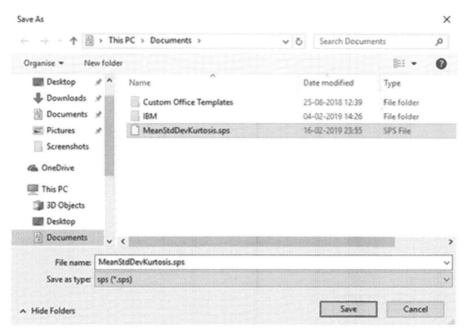

Select Save to save the Syntax file

If you want to run the analysis for the same dataset over and over again, all you have to do is open the Syntax file in SPSS and select this option highlighted in red:

Select the Run Syntax icon to run the analysis again

Of course, if you want to run the same analysis for another dataset, then you have to just change the variable name, as shown below:

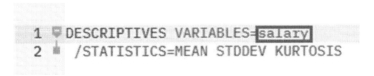

Changed the Variable name from ComputerSystems to salary

Run the syntax file on the dataset that has this variable and you should obtain the output for the mean, standard deviation, and kurtosis.

See, it's really simple!

But what if you want to write these SPSS Syntax commands yourself?

How to write SPSS Syntax commands yourself...

In order for you to write these Syntax commands yourself, you need to know what keywords are used to create a list of Syntax commands that will work just as well as being able to point-and-click through menus.

For this, you have to access the URL to the Command Syntax Reference where you will find a list of commands, as we discussed in an earlier chapter.

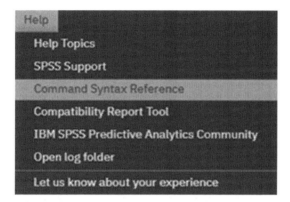

Select the Command Syntax Reference option

Please note that if you have little or no programming experience, it might take a while. Make sure you save the code for every procedure you would like to repeat and alter it for other datasets.

Over time, you should be able to open a new Syntax file and write out these commands yourself.

In Closing

We have covered the absolute basics of saving and running Syntax commands. As far as our discussion goes on SPSS features, we are about done. Just one more thing: as soon as you are familiar with SPSS Syntax, you can try integrating Python 2 or 3 with this awesome software package.

Final Thoughts

Let's admit one thing: SPSS is daunting to use at first. However, given that its functions are available for both descriptive and inferential statistics, one can truly use this tool to improve their knowledge in Statistics as a whole, but also to use the power of technology to compute large amounts of data with ease.

Imagine having a tool that helps you calculate the mean of a variable but also perform hypothetical testing as well. That's how SPSS works.

You can throw that calculator out!

While this book has served to help beginners learn statistics from the ground up, it has also attempted to help learners use SPSS in order to apply all statistical concepts learned. As simply as possible. Or at least, this has been the objective given that statistics can get confusing as we move towards inferential statistics.

So, let's take the opportunity to summarize this effort of learning both SPSS and statistics in one go. Not only did we cover measures of descriptive statistics but we also learned how to use them with real-life but simple datasets. In addition, we also tried to understand what each and every feature in SPSS can help you with, right from the File to the Help Menus. Of course, one cannot forget how important it is to create good charts that can reveal a lot based on the data that you are using for your analysis.

An SPSS chapter after a Statistics theory chapter was placed intentionally for you to apply the very concepts learned before but in a gradual and step-by-step manner.

We also tried to understand certain concepts and procedures used in Inferential Statistics ranging from One Sample T-Tests to Correlation Analysis. What was out of the scope of this book was complex statistical analyses, as it would have proven to be detrimental to your learning of the basics. That said, it is really up to you to take this study of statistics to the next level, given that there are a number of scholarly resources available over the internet and at your local university.

There's a lot of free resources to learn Data Analysis over the internet

As you know by now, the Analyze menu is probably the most important amongst the lot, even if one can use features contained in other menus to speed up and automate their data analysis. Of course, familiarity with these features can only improve over time, which is why one must endeavour to continue to use SPSS as much as possible. Feel free to use this guide to help you with the features, as some of them have been moved around or changed completely since version 25 was released.

Given how data science requires one to constantly learn and adapt to new methods, it's only in your best interests to go over each of these features in the next few months. This is true about the study of statistics as well, where theoretical concepts will require constant application. You never know when you might need a range of techniques to test a hypothesis.

You can begin this by looking for qualitative and quantitative data. There's enough to be found everywhere these days. Whether it is the weather, sales and marketing, medicine, politics, law enforcement, you name it. Messing around with different types of data will make it interesting and fun, too.

Yes, lots of qualitative data in a library, for sure!

As fun as this task will be, developing that statistical bent-of-mind will help us to not only collect good data, but also to learn how to use it intelligently with such a powerful tool at our disposal. Better still, if you can learn how to use Syntax commands and save them for future use, this will reduce the amount of effort and time you have to put in, especially as you progress to more complex types of data analysis.

In saying that, it will be great if this guide helped you find your way around SPSS while greatly reducing the discomfort that comes with learning a new software package for whatever reason. Even if SPSS might prove a bit difficult to learn, there are features that give it a clear edge over the competition. There's just nothing like this tool on the market at the moment, thanks to the years that have gone into keeping it updated or these times that we live in.

Speaking of which, it would be lovely to consider learning both the languages of both Python and R, as bonafide data analysts consider this to be a must if you're just getting started with data analysis and data science.

Finally, I would like to leave you with a quote by Lao Tzu, who said that a journey of a thousand miles begins with a single step.

Michelangelo, at 87 said that he was still learning

In reading this book, you've done just that. Never stop learning. Never stop improving. For the race to perfection really has no finish line!

Bibliography

Academic Texts

Isotala, J. (n.d.). *Basics of Statistics*. Tampere, Finland: University of Tampere.

Lane, D.M. (n.d.). *Introduction to Statistics*. Houston, TX: Rice University.

McCormick, K & Salcedo, J. (2015). *SPSS for Dummies (3rd ed.)*. Hoboken, NJ: Wiley Publishing.

Yakir, B. (2011). *Introduction to Statistical Thinking (With R, without Calculus)*. Jerusalem, Israel: The Hebrew University.

Almquist, Y.B., Ashir, S. & Brännström, L. (n.d.). *A Guide to Quantitative Methods*. Stockholm, Sweden: Stockholm University.

Online Sources

Anderson, D.R., Sweeney, D.J., & Williams, T.A. (2019). Statistics. *Encyclopædia Britannica*. Retrieved from https://www.britannica.com/science/statistics

About SPSS Inc. (2009). *IBM SPSS.* Retrieved from http://www.spss.com.hk/corpinfo/history.htm

Bose, B. (2018). Top 10 Python Libraries for Data Science in 2018. *Digital Vidya.* Retrieved from https://www.digitalvidya.com/blog/top-10-python-libraries-for-data-science/

What is SPSS and How Does It Work? (2019). *Educba.* Retrieved from https://www.educba.com/what-is-spss-and-how-does-it-work/

IBM SPSS Statistics. (2019). *IBM.* Retrieved from https://www.ibm.com/products/spss-statistics

IBM SPSS Statistics Desktop 25.0.0.0. (n.d.). *IBM.* Retrieved from https://www.hearne.software/getattachment/03761183-bc74-420e-984d-8ee688b80af0/SPSS-Statistics-v25-System-Requirements-Windows.aspx

SeattleDataGuy. (2018). 7 Use Cases For Data Science And Predictive Analytics. *Towards Data Science.* Retrieved from https://towardsdatascience.com/7-use-cases-for-data-science-and-predictive-analytics-e3616e9331f9

Bobriakov, I. (2018). Top 7 Data Science Use Cases in Healthcare. *ActiveWizards.* Retrieved from https://medium.com/activewizards-machine-learning-company/top-7-data-science-use-cases-in-healthcare-cddfa82fd9e3

Petersen, R. (2019). 37 Big Data Case Studies with Big Results. *Businesses Grow.* Retrieved from https://businessesgrow.com/2016/12/06/big-data-case-studies/

Data. (2019). *Merriam-Webster Dictionary.* Retrieved from https://www.merriam-webster.com/dictionary/data

Raw data. (2019). *Wikipedia.* Retrieved from https://en.wikipedia.org/wiki/Raw_data

Bhat, A. (2019). Quantitative Data: Definition, Types, Analysis and Examples. *QuestionPro.* Retrieved from https://www.questionpro.com/blog/quantitative-data/

McLeod, S. (2017). What's the difference between qualitative and quantitative research? *Simply Psychology.* Retrieved from https://www.simplypsychology.org/qualitative-quantitative.html

Summarising and Presenting Data. (2019). *SurfStat Australia.* Retrieved from https://surfstat.anu.edu.au/surfstat-home/1-1-1.html

Minitab Blog Editor. (2017). Understanding Qualitative, Quantitative, Attribute, Discrete, and Continuous Data Types. *The Minitab Blog.* Retrieved from http://blog.minitab.com/blog/understanding-statistics/understanding-qualitative-quantitative-attribute-discrete-and-continuous-data-types

Anatasia. (2017). Overview of Qualitative And Quantitative Data Collection Methods. *Cleverism.* Retrieved from https://www.cleverism.com/qualitative-and-quantitative-data-collection-methods/

Utsav, G. (n.d.). Data Cleansing | Introduction. *Geeks for Geeks.* Retrieved from https://www.geeksforgeeks.org/data-cleansing-introduction/

Ma, X., Hummer, D., Golden, J.J., Fox, P.A., Hazen, R.M., Morrison, S.M., Downs, R.T., Madhikarmi, B.L., Wang, C., & Meyer, M.B. (2017). Using Visual Exploratory Data Analysis to Facilitate Collaboration and Hypothesis Generation in Cross-Disciplinary Research. *International Journal of Geo-Information*, 6(11), 368. https://doi.org/10.3390/ijgi6110368

Valcheva, S. (n.d.). Qualitative vs Quantitative Data: Definitions, Analysis, Examples. *Intellspot.* Retrieved from http://intellspot.com/qualitative-vs-quantitative-data/

Types of Data & Measurement Scales: Nominal, Ordinal, Interval and Ratio. (2019). *My Market Research Methods.* Retrieved from https://www.mymarketresearchmethods.com/types-of-data-nominal-ordinal-interval-ratio/

IBM SPSS Statistics Subscription - New documentation. (2019). *IBM SPSS Statistics.* Retrieved from https://spsssub.ibm.com/docs/content/SSLVMB_subs/statistics_kc_ddita_cloud/spss/product_landing_cloud.html?context=analytics

Descriptive and Inferential Statistics. (2018). *Laerd Statistics.* Retrieved from https://statistics.laerd.com/statistical-guides/descriptive-inferential-statistics.php

Normal Distribution. (n.d.). *University of Connecticut.* Retrieved from https://researchbasics.education.uconn.edu/normal-distribution/#

Sullivan, L. & LaMorte, W.W. (2016). InterQuartile Range (IQR). *Boston University.* Retrieved from http://sphweb.bumc.bu.edu/otlt/mph-modules/bs/bs704_summarizingdata/bs704_summarizingdata7.html

Measures of Shape. (2013). *Australian Bureau of Statistics.* Retrieved from http://www.abs.gov.au/websitedbs/a3121120.nsf/home/statistical+language+-+measures+of+shape

Donges, N. (2018). Intro to Descriptive Statistics. *Towards Data Science.* Retrieved from https://towardsdatascience.com/intro-to-descriptive-statistics-252e9c464ac9

Chapter 1: Descriptive Statistics and the Normal Distribution. (n.d.). *ER Services.* Retrieved from https://courses.lumenlearning.com/suny-natural-resources-biometrics/chapter/chapter-1-descriptive-statistics-and-the-normal-distribution/

Statistics Dictionary. (2019). *Stat Trek.* Retrieved from https://stattrek.com/statistics/dictionary.aspx?definition=interquartile%20range

Measures of Central Tendency. (2018). *Laerd Statistics.* Retrieved from https://statistics.laerd.com/statistical-guides/measures-central-tendency-mean-mode-median.php

Gardner, M. (n.d.). Statistics - A Guide. *Data Analytics.* Retrieved from http://www.dataanalytics.org.uk/Data%20Analysis/Statistics/summarizing-data.htm#shape_statistics

Jain, D. (2018). Skew and Kurtosis: 2 Important Statistics terms you need to know in Data Science. *Code Burst.* Retrieved from https://codeburst.io/2-important-statistics-terms-you-need-to-know-in-data-science-skewness-and-kurtosis-388fef94eeaa

French, K. (n.d.). Why Your Brain Loves Visual Content [Infographic]. *Column Five Media.* Retrieved from https://www.columnfivemedia.com/why-your-brain-loves-visual-content-infographic

Slutsky, D.J. (2014). The Effective Use of Graphs. *Journal of Wrist Surgery*, 3(2), 67-68. https://10.1055/s-0034-1375704

Measures of Skewness and Kurtosis. (2013). *NIST SEMATECH.* Retrieved from https://www.itl.nist.gov/div898/handbook/eda/section3/eda35b.htm

Helmenstine, T. (2018). What Is the Difference Between Independent and Dependent Variables? *ThoughtCo.* Retrieved from https://www.thoughtco.com/independent-and-dependent-variables-differences-606115

Taylor, C. (2018). 7 Graphs Commonly Used in Statistics. *ThoughtCo.* Retrieved from https://www.thoughtco.com/frequently-used-statistics-graphs-4158380

Line Graph. (2019). *SmartDraw.* Retrieved from
https://www.smartdraw.com/line-graph/

Collecting Data. (2019). *BBC Skillswise.* Retrieved from
http://www.bbc.co.uk/skillswise/factsheet/ma35data-l1-f-collecting-and-representing-data-using-line-graphs

Galarynk, M. (2018). Understanding Boxplots. *Towards Data Science.* Retrieved from https://towardsdatascience.com/understanding-boxplots-5e2df7bcbd51

Standard Score. (2018). *Laerd Statistics.* Retrieved from
https://statistics.laerd.com/statistical-guides/standard-score.php

Z-Score: Definition, Formula and Calculation. (2019). *Statistics How To.* Retrieved from
https://www.statisticshowto.datasciencecentral.com/probability-and-statistics/z-score/

Z-table (Right of Curve or Left). (2019). *Statistics How To.* Retrieved from
https://www.statisticshowto.datasciencecentral.com/tables/z-table/

Brown, S. (2011). *Measures of Shape: Skewness and Kurtosis.* Retrieved from
http://web.ipac.caltech.edu/staff/fmasci/home/astro_refs/SkewStatSignif.pdf

Chapter 3 Evaluating the Characteristics of Data. (2016). *SAGE Publishing.* Retrieved from https://us.sagepub.com/sites/default/files/upm-binaries/70453_Pett_Chapter_3.pdf

Case Summaries. (2019). *IBM Knowledge Center.* Retrieved from https://www.ibm.com/support/knowledgecenter/en/SSLVMB_subs/statistics_mainhelp_ddita/spss/base/idh_summ.html

Line Graphs. (2017). *Math Goodies.* Retrieved from https://www.mathgoodies.com/lessons/graphs/line

Multiple Line Graphs. (2019). *CK-12.* Retrieved from https://www.ck12.org/statistics/multiple-line-graphs/lesson/Multiple-Line-Graphs-MSM7/

How to Analyze a Line Graph. (n.d.). *SAISD Social Studies Department.* Retrieved from https://www.saisd.net/admin/curric/sstudies/resources/teacher_zone/skills/howto_line_graph.pdf

Population Pyramid. (n.d.). *The Data Visualisation Catalogue.* Retrieved from https://datavizcatalogue.com/methods/population_pyramid.html

Parallel Coordinates Plot. (n.d.). *The Data Visualisation Catalogue.* Retrieved from https://datavizcatalogue.com/methods/parallel_coordinates.html

Why It Matters: Probability and Probability Distributions. (n.d.). *Lumen Candela.* Retrieved from https://courses.lumenlearning.com/wmopen-concepts-statistics/chapter/introduction-6/

Sampling Distribution of the Mean. (n.d.). Retrieved from http://www.skidmore.edu/~hfoley/Handouts/Samp.Dist.pdf

Distribution of Sample Means (1 of 4). (n.d.). *Lumen Candela.* Retrieved from https://courses.lumenlearning.com/wmopen-concepts-statistics/chapter/distribution-of-sample-means-1-of-4/

Williams, T.A., Sweeney, D.J., Anderson, D.R., Gaur, A., Higgins, J., Lotha, G., Sampaolo, M & The Editors of Encyclopaedia Britannica. Random variables and probability distributions. *Encyclopædia Britannica.* Retrieved from https://www.britannica.com/science/statistics/Random-variables-and-probability-distributions#ref367442

The Editors of Encyclopaedia Britannica. (2016). Point estimation. *Encyclopædia Britannica.* Retrieved from https://www.britannica.com/science/point-estimation

Estimator. (2019). *Wikipedia.* Retrieved from https://en.wikipedia.org/wiki/Estimator

Stephanie. (2016). Population Proportion. *Statistics How To.* Retrieved from https://www.statisticshowto.datasciencecentral.com/population-proportion/

Central Limit Theorem: Definition and Examples in Easy Steps. (2019). *Statistics How To.* Retrieved from https://www.statisticshowto.datasciencecentral.com/probability-and-statistics/normal-distributions/central-limit-theorem-definition-examples/

Point Estimates and Confidence Intervals. (n.d.). *CQE Academy.* Retrieved from http://www.cqeacademy.com/cqe-body-of-knowledge/quantitative-methods-tools/point-estimates-and-confidence-intervals/

Kenton, W. (2018). Statistically Significant. *Investopedia.* Retrieved from https://www.investopedia.com/terms/s/statistically_significant.asp

Rumsey, D.J. (2019). What a p-Value Tells You about Statistical Data. *Dummies.* Retrieved from https://www.dummies.com/education/math/statistics/what-a-p-value-tells-you-about-statistical-data/

One-Sample T-Test using SPSS Statistics. (n.d.). *Laerd Statistics.* Retrieved from https://statistics.laerd.com/spss-tutorials/one-sample-t-test-using-spss-statistics.php

Jones, J. (2019). Hypothesis Testing with SPSS. *Richland College Community.* Retrieved from https://people.richland.edu/james/lecture/spss/testing/

Foley, B. (2018). What is Regression Analysis and Why Should I Use It? *Survey Gizmo.* Retrieved from https://www.surveygizmo.com/resources/blog/regression-analysis/

broadcasttom10 [Screen name]. 2015, January 11). Estimation and Confidence Intervals in SPSS [Video file]. Retrieved from https://www.youtube.com/watch?v=8LnvZB9IWJw

Images

Froztbyte. (Photographer). (2010). *The logo of SPSS* [Digital Image]. Retrieved from https://commons.wikimedia.org/wiki/File:SPSS_logo.svg

Felsenburgh, J. (Photographer). (2013). *Karl Pearson, 1910* [Digital Image]. Retrieved from https://commons.wikimedia.org/wiki/File:Karl_Pearson,_1910.jpg

Wills, T. (Photographer). (2013). *Card puncher - NARA - 513295* [Digital Image]. Retrieved from https://en.wikipedia.org/wiki/File:Card_puncher_-_NARA_-_513295.jpg

Hammond, C (Photographer). (n.d.). *FORTRAN The Pioneering Programming Language* [Digital Image]. IBM. Retrieved from https://www.ibm.com/ibm/history/ibm100/us/en/icons/fortran/impacts/

Harris, D. (Photographer). (2019). *Math Hurts: Risks of Predictive Analytics for Small Businesses* [Digital Image]. Software Advice. Retrieved from https://www.softwareadvice.com/resources/predictive-analytics-for-small-business/

marketingapponfly (Photographer). (2016). *IBM SPSS Statistics Base on AppOnFly* [Digital Image]! Windows Remote Desktop. Retrieved from https://windowsremotedesktopcom.wordpress.com/2016/01/08/ibm-spss-statistics-base-on-apponfly-2/

Stevens, J (Photographer). (2018). *How to choose between R and Python for careers in data science* [Digital Image]. Working Nation. Retrieved from https://workingnation.com/r-python-data-science-careers/

McZusatz (Photographer). (2017). *Matlab Logo* [Digital Image]. Wikiversity. Retrieved from https://en.wikiversity.org/wiki/File:Matlab_Logo.png

Ringstrom, D (Photographer). (2016). *An Easier Way to Open CSV Files in Excel* [Digital Image]. Accounting Web. Retrieved from https://www.accountingweb.com/technology/excel/an-easier-way-to-open-csv-files-in-excel

Hamrick, C. (Photographer). (2016). *Stop Touching the Hot Stove* [Digital Image]. Daily PS. Retrieved from https://dailyps.com/stop-touching-the-hot-stove/

Barman, S. (Photographer). (2010). *Konrad Zuse - Inventor of Modern Computer* [Digital Image]. Code Pen. Retrieved from https://codepen.io/shuvongkor/full/bMLgxx

Valcheva, S. (Photographer). (n.d.). *Qualitative vs Quantitative Data: Definitions, Analysis, Examples*. Intellspot. Retrieved from http://intellspot.com/qualitative-vs-quantitative-data/

Made in the USA
San Bernardino, CA
11 May 2019